5/11/87

Mayor —

We're always trying to promote Norwalk. See page 90 & 139.

By the way, this is a fabulous book.

Your friend,

Stew

Earl Nightingale's

Greatest Discovery

The PMA Book Series
W. Clement Stone, General Editor
Robert C. Anderson, Editorial Consultant

This series of books presents practical approaches to achieving success and fulfillment
in business, professional, and personal life.

Based on the proposition that there is an
intelligent solution to every human problem
and that with a positive mental attitude
(PMA) a person can overcome any adversity,
each book in this series offers practical, step-
by-step advice and inspiration to action.

*Earl Nightingale's Greatest Discovery: "The
Strangest Secret. . . Revisited"* is the first book in
this series.

Upcoming Titles:
   W. Clement Stone's New Formula for Success,
Samuel Cypert
The Goal Seeker, Jerry Baker

Published by Dodd, Mead & Company, Inc.
71 Fifth Avenue, New York, New York 10003
Distributed in Canada by
McClelland and Stewart Limited, Toronto.
Manufactured in the United States of America.
Interior design and production supervision by Nick Scelsi
First Edition

1 2 3 4 5 6 7 8 9 10

Library of Congress Cataloging-in-Publication Data

Nightingale, Earl.
Earl Nightingale's greatest discovery.

(The PMA book series)
Includes index.
1. Success. I. Title. II. Series.
BF637.S8N49   1987   158'.1   87-424
ISBN 0-396-08928-3

Earl Nightingale's

Greatest Discovery

"The Strangest Secret... Revisited"

Dodd, Mead & Company
New York

*For Diana—as the earth
thanks the sun*

Contents

Foreword

While vacationing with my family in Hawaii I received a long–distance telephone call from my secretary. "I know that you told me to keep all business matters strictly on hold until you return," she said, "but I just knew that you would want to have this message."

"I sure hope it is important," I responded, "because I do not want to even think about anything for the next few weeks."

"You received a telephone call from Earl Nightingale," she informed me "He wants you to write the foreword for his book, *Earl Nightingale's Greatest Discovery: "The Strangest Secret. . . Revisited."* I was sure you would want to know that right away since you've always talked so enthusiastically about the importance of his message, and you listen to that tape every week."

Five minutes later I was on the telephone to Earl and when we finished our conversation I said to my wife, "Can you imagine, Earl Nightingale, the author of *The Strangest Secret,* actually wants me to write the foreword for his book. This is one of the greatest honors of my life."

You see, the content of *The Strangest Secret* has been a source of inspiration for me for as long as I can remember. Somehow the words on that beautiful little recording solidified a philosophy of life that I had always practiced, yet had never seen articulated in print or on a recording. I have recommended to many of my clients over the years, listen to *The Strangest Secret,* I have told my children, listen to *The Strangest Secret,* my business associates, friends, clerks, and even total strangers who seem to need a shining beam of truth in their lives. Always the advice is the same—listen to *The*

Strangest Secret. Listen carefully and come back to me with how you think the message might apply to you. So, you can well imagine my state of excitement when I heard the words—Earl Nightingale wants you to write the foreword for his book—*Earl Nightingale's Greatest Discovery: "The Strangest Secret. . . Revisited."*

As honored and thrilled as I was to have Earl ask me to say something here in the pages of this magnificent book, somehow it seems fitting. For all of my life I have been blessed with this marvelous gift of knowing the importance of *The Strangest Secret.* I have used it since I was a little boy. I have applied the essential messages of this book throughout all the days of my life, and parlayed the essential ingredients of the "strangest secret" into any and all success I have ever enjoyed. I have lived *The Strangest Secret* since I first showed up on this planet in 1940, and Earl's recording, and now his long–overdue book are the instruments which have illustrated to me most vividly—"Yes, that's it. I've been doing it this way all along and it really works." For me, Wayne Dyer, Earl's contributions have been the exclamation point on a lifetime of living by my own inner signals. For many others, Earl provides a glorious road map for how to get out of the self-imposed rut that they may have created for themselves.

It matters not how you use Earl's recordings and this book, just the fact that the information is now in print makes me feel that many many people will be able to benefit and use the "strangest secret" in ways based upon where they are on the path of their own enlightenment. And as Earl states so fittingly, "We are here only to serve others," and serve others he has done for a lifetime. But somehow, with the publication of this book, Earl's lifetime of serving is now fixed in permanence. The library shelves of the world will now house *Earl Nightingale's Greatest Discovery.* Inquisitive children still unborn, will leaf through the pages of this gem in a future generation or even a future millenium. It is now where it has always belonged: available for everyone, in all languages, in a form that will last forever. A recording is a magnificent way to experience a piece of truth and beauty, but a book is something to curl up with, to open on a long airplane ride, or to keep handy as a reference during a particularly troublesome time. Obviously, I am ecstatic that Earl has put his message into this format. It deserves to be a BOOK!

When I was a very young boy, a woman once told me three words that literally sum up the message of *Earl Nightingale's Greatest Discovery.* She said, "Wayne, if you don't want something bad to happen, or if you want good things for yourself in your life, be careful about what you think, for you will become what you think as sure as the dawn follows night. Always remember, THOUGHTS ARE THINGS!" Wow — the entire world wrapped up in those three magic words — THOUGHTS ARE THINGS! Think hard on this as you read the pages of Earl's book. A thought is the most powerful force in the universe. You can make of your life whatever you wish if you learn to make your thoughts work for you.

Today, workshops are conducted all over the country on Creative Imagery, Visualization, Self-talk, Success-Imagery, Positive Affirmations, and the like. Volumes are being written on the subject, and even hard–core scientists and pragmatic diehards in all fields are beginning to explore this realm of *thought* as a vehicle for transformation. In education, business, religion, medicine and virtually all fields of human exploration, the emphasis is now shifting to the importance of attitude and thought. Business leaders spend millions on training their workers to use their creative thinking capacities and attitudes to improve the bottom line. Medical schools, that once scorned the idea of the mind as healer, now offer specialized courses in wellness training and visualization as adjuncts to the entire healing process. Educators are redirecting their efforts to help young people to understand the significance of their "self-talk" in the formation of their self-images, and ultimately their success in life. The focus is now, more than ever, on how one thinks and uses his unlimited potential for positive–attitude development to create the kind of existence one desires. All of this "new thought" or "new age" thinking originated in the concepts that Earl Nightingale recorded and has now written in this book. *Thoughts Are Things!* Positive thoughts create a positive image, and soon the individual will act upon those images, rather than the negative, self-defeating thoughts that previously filled one's consciousness. *Being* healthy is a function of first *thinking* healthy. The *will* to live is nothing more than a *thought* to live. The *belief* in one's abilities is nothing more than a *thought* in one's abilities. The *perseverance* to push onward is nothing more than the thought to push onward. The *expectation* of happiness is nothing more than the *thought* of happiness. The *desire* to be loved is nothing more than the *thought* to be loved. Indeed, it all boils down to THOUGHT.

While some may say that it is too simple to say that thought controls everything, nevertheless, for me it is crystal clear. We in fact become what we think about each and every day. I believe so strongly in this message that I take it several steps further. It is my belief that once we remove all the junk inside of us, that is the hate, anger, fear, depression, anxiety, stress and so on, we then open ourselves up for unlimited use of our thinking abilities. When we are clear inside — or centered if you will — thinking miracles begin to occur. We can think our way to levels never before even imagined while so filled with the junk. And how do we rid ourselves of that inner junkpile? By acknowledging that it only gets there through thought in the first place. There is no stress in the world, only people thinking stressfully. There is no anxiety in our world, only people thinking anxiously. The logic is irrefutable. Thought creates our inner world, and thought can eradicate that which we have created which is self-defeating. How does one do it? By taking charge of how one elects to think each and every moment, one day at a time. The habit of thinking in healthful productive ways can replace the habit of thinking in self-condemning ways. In this book, Earl makes it easy for us to see specifically how to make our minds works for us; to become what we choose through thought. I have never seen it written more succinctly, nor have I read it stated in a more readable style.

Earl Nightingale's great gift to millions of us over the years has been his ability to communicate seemingly complex matters in a commonsense listenable way. His very brief broadcast required him to get to the point and eliminate all of the oatmeal. Those thousands and thousands of five–minute spots provided Earl with the discipline for getting to it. As you read through this eminently readable volume, you will see the effects of those years. The precision is right here in every page. The uncounted "AH HAs" will astound you. Most books in the "self-development" field are manuals to study, much like a reference text. Believe it or not, this book is a page-turner, a rarity indeed in this field. Just like you can't wait to hear the rest of one of Earl's radio spots, here you will find yourself wanting to read more. Earl has combined philosophy, psychology, sociology, and his love for the English Language with his plain old-fashioned horse sense, and created what I am absolutely certain will be a classic in its own field. He has created his own genre, his own format, and it will defy compartmentalization. It is uniquely Earl Nightingale. Just like his recordings have the specialized stamp of a one-of-a-kind presentation, with his immediately recognizable gravelly voice, a blending of quotations from the masters, and his own common sense from having been "dragged up" through the suffering and stench of poverty, so, too, does this book have the Nightingale stamp of uniqueness. It is all here: the stories that capture your imagination, the philosophy that is timeless, the wisdom born of having lived through it, and the remarkable advice that can transform your life if you so choose. This book, like its classic predecessor in the audio format, is like a warm shower running inside of me. It feels right, it is comforting, and it also is an instrument for cleansing. I am proud to have shared a few of my thoughts in the opening pages of this jewel. While I am mighty proud of my many books and recordings in the entire field of human development, I must say that many of the ideas in those products had their original seeds sown in the simple logic and the powerful words of *Earl Nightingale's Greatest Discovery*.

As you read through the pages of this book, keep in mind those powerful words that I heard as a very young boy: *Thoughts Are Things*. For indeed, if you can get hold of this idea, and take total control of your own free will to think as you choose, and then take action on those new and self-serving thoughts, you will not only transform your own life, but you will begin to impact in the same way on those around you. And ultimately, it is only through a change in consciousness (thought) that the entire world will be transformed. Such is the impact of this critically important book. A thought can transform you, those immediately around you, and the entire world as well.

Thank you, Earl, for putting your life-changing thoughts down on paper, and for thinking of me to be a small part of your contribution, I can only say I am honored — and that is no secret!

Dr. Wayne W. Dyer
Author, *Your Erroneous Zones*

Introduction

I began looking for the secret of success when I was twelve years old. I found it at the age of twenty-nine. That was in 1950. In the spring of 1956, I was asked to put the essence of what I had learned during those many years of assiduous reading and research into a rather short essay. Because my working career involved both writing and broadcasting, I was to then record the essay for the possible benefit of others.

I thought about it, turning the ideas over and over in my mind. Finally, I asked myself, "What would you tell your children if you found you had only a short time to live? What advice could you pass on to them that would assist them in living highly productive, very successful lives?" I awakened at four the next morning with the answer to that question clearly in mind.

I got up, put on a pot of coffee, and went into my study to put my thoughts on paper. By ten that morning I had completed the essay. I showered and dressed and by noon was recording my essay at CBS. It was finished before lunch. I called what I had written and recorded *The Strangest Secret*.

First on tape, then on a ten-inch record, *The Strangest Secret* was the child that grew into the audio recording industry. With no effort on my part whatsoever, with no advertising of any kind, *The Strangest Secret* became a national best–seller. I was ill-prepared to handle the avalanche of orders for that recording. My good friend Lloyd Conant, then owner of Specialty Mail Services in Chicago, stepped into the breach. He was happy and abundantly prepared to handle the business end of my sudden good fortune. The orders continued to pour in from every section of the country. It was astonishing how the word about that recorded message got around. And that was the beginning of what was to become—officially in 1960—the Nightingale–Conant Corporation of Chicago.

Before very long my good friend Dick Hutter, then head of Columbia Records in Chicago, told us we had earned a gold record for sales exceeding one million copies. And even today, as I write this introduction in the early fall of 1986, *The Strangest Secret* still sells. The many recorded programs for which it paved the way are selling to hundreds of thousands of people all over the Free World in the form of tape cassettes.

Now it is time to write this book. I found the secret for which I had searched so long and diligently in a book. Books remain to this day one of my overriding loves. My home is filled with them; they form double rows on the shelves of my study because we don't have enough bookshelves to properly display them. While nothing can take the place of a tape cassette for a person commuting to and from work in an automobile, books will no doubt remain, for centuries perhaps, the world's great source of knowledge and enjoyment. Everything we learn and enjoy in knowledge and entertainment begins with the written word. It is in printed form before it becomes anything else. So was *The Strangest Secret* and the ideas that went into it.

Now, thirty years later, it's time to look back over the intervening years. It's time to revisit *The Strangest Secret* and examine, or reexamine, our journey into meaning.

How can I possibly thank those who have helped me in my efforts? They line the shelves of my study and can be found all over our home. Those men and women who took the time and mustered the patience to put their ideas, their knowledge into books for you and me. They go back to the shadowy Lao Tse and to the Bible, and they are as modern as Wayne Dyer and Tom Peters and all the fine authors published in audio (and printed) form by my company. They would certainly include my late wonderful friend Lloyd Conant and all the people who work with such loving care in our company in Chicago. Dick Hutter, formerly of Columbia Records and now happily ensconced as head of his own production company, has been of great help to me and has as well kept me up to date on the latest funny story. In mentioning these people, I know I'm leaving out far too many.

I must give very special thanks to Diana, my wife, without whose love and laughter, sound thinking, and perseverance this book would not have been written at all. She filled my life with love, laughter, and sunshine at a very critical time, and she continues to do so to my everlasting joy.

I want to give special thanks to my good friend Bob Anderson of PMA Books for his scholarly and wise editing and for his excellent advice and to Lynne Lumsden and Jon Harden, the owners and guiding lights of Dodd, Mead & Company, Inc., my publisher. They're delightful people with a genuine love for the fine work they are doing in the publishing industry. It's good to know that one of the oldest publishing companies in New York is also one of the youngest in attitude and outlook.

And now let me thank you, without whom nothing happens. Nothing at all. As my old friend Red Motley always said, "Nothing happens until somebody sells something!"

CHAPTER I

The Discovery

In order to fully enjoy prosperity and its accompanying sense of achievement, one needs to have known poverty and an environment in which daily survival is the purpose of life. As a youngster, I didn't know anything about a sense of achievement, but I was all too aware of being poor. It didn't seem to bother the other kids, but it bothered me. What made it all the more exasperating to me, as a boy of twelve, was to be poor in Southern California, where there seemed to be so many who were rich. In fact, anyone who had an automobile, an electric refrigerator and wall-to-wall carpeting was rich in my book, and the children of such people seemed to me to be fortunate indeed. I decided to find out why some people were rich while so very many of us were poor.

The year was 1933—the bottom of the Great Depression. Millions were unemployed. My two brothers and I were fortunate; although our father had disappeared in search of greener pastures, our mother never missed a day at her WPA sewing–factory job. Her earnings, I recall, were fifty-five dollars a month, which produced survival. We lived in "Tent City" behind the old Mariner Apartments on the waterfront in Long Beach, California.

"What makes the difference?" I asked myself. "Why are some people well off financially and others poor? Why are some so well paid while others are so poorly paid? What's the difference? What's going on here?"

I tried asking the adults who lived in our neighborhood and soon discovered they didn't know any more than I did. In fact I made what was to me an astonishing discovery: The adults in our neighborhood didn't know anything at all. They were pitifully uneducated—driven by instinct, other-directed.

My mother had many endearing qualities. One was her unfailing good cheer; another was her love of books. She haunted the public library, and my fondest memory of her is of her eating oatmeal and milk early in the morning under a dangling, naked, underpowered light bulb with a book propped up in front of her. She loved travel books, especially. Never able to travel herself, she explored the earth from pole to pole through her books on travel and adventure. I'm sure it helped save her sanity during those hard years. She was an attractive woman, still young but completely dedicated to the raising of her boys. Her books and our battered radio were her only entertainment. She read on the long Pacific Electric train rides to and from work in Los Angeles and after we boys had gone to bed at night. On weekends, after cleaning and doing the laundry, her books again filled her world with exciting travel and high adventure. Later in life, I realized that she never had to stand in a sweltering customs shed, or see her luggage disappear into three Italian taxis, or struggle with a foreign language or currency, yet she had traveled from one end of the earth to the other and was intimate with the most remote places on the planet. That she was able to do so without ever leaving Los Angeles County was a tribute to the excellent public library system. It didn't cost her a dime.

And so it was to the Long Beach Public Library that I went seeking the elusive secret of success. I didn't know where to look among those thousands of titles, but I felt sure it was there somewhere. It seemed to me that if anyone had ever figured it out, he would surely have written a book about it. After I began my search, I soon found myself sidetracked into the world of the most exciting fiction: the Hardy Boys, the great mind-expanding stories of Edgar Rice Burroughs, and the Westerns of Zane Grey. Then came the fascinating stories of the Plains Indians by Stanley Vestal, and before I knew it I was as addicted to books as my mother. I learned about the importance of honesty, personal integrity, and courage and of believing in what is right and being willing to fight for it. I know that it was my early love affair with books that resulted in my getting a better-than-average education.

Later, as World War II loomed on the horizon, I left school and enlisted in the Marine Corps. But I continued my studies. I read everything I could lay my hands on.

I made two decisions that guided the remainder of my life. The first was to discover the secret of success. The second was to become a writer. I loved books and wanted to write them myself. Toward the end of the war I found myself back in the States working as an instructor at Camp Lejeune, North Carolina. Driving between the base and nearby Jacksonville, I noticed a radio station under construction. I decided to apply for an announcing job, working nights and weekends. I auditioned and was hired. Sitting before the microphone at that small radio station, WJNC Jacksonville, North Carolina, was the beginning of my radio career. The owner-manager, Lester Gould, and I became good friends.

I took to broadcasting like nothing before in my life. I was in my element, and more than forty years later, I'm still in it. But my desire to write did not lessen, and gradually I began planning for the day when I would write my own programs. In the meantime, I learned the business, doing commercials, news, and station breaks. It was extra income and would prove to be valuable experience after I was mustered out of the Marine Corps.

My reading and search for the secret of success continued without letup. I studied the world's great religions. I found myself especially fascinated with philosophy and psychology. But it wasn't until one weekend when I was twenty-nine and working for CBS in Chicago that enlightenment came. While reading, it suddenly dawned upon me that I had been reading the same truth over and over again for many years. I had read it in the New Testament, in the sayings of Buddha, in the writings of Lao Tse, in the works of Emerson. And all of a sudden, there they were, the words, in the proper order that I had been looking for for seventeen years. The astonishing truth that *we become what we think about.*

It was as if I were suddenly immersed in a bright light. Of course! I remember sitting bolt upright at the thought of the simplicity of it. That was what Ortega was talking about when he reminded us that we are the only creatures on earth born into a natural state of disorientation with our world. It had to be because we are the only creatures with the godlike power to create our own worlds. And we do. We do create our own worlds all the years of our lives. We become what we think about most of the time. And if we don't think at all—which seemed to have been the principal problem of the people back in my old Long Beach neighborhood— we don't become anything at all.

There it was, just six words. There are more than six hundred thousand words in the English language, but those were the six I had searched for, in that particular order, ever since the age of twelve. Seventeen years it had taken to see the obvious. How could we become anything else? Our minds are the steering mechanisms of our lives. And each of us who does much thinking at all thinks differently. There at last was the secret of success or failure or something in between. Each of us is sentenced to become what he or she thinks about. Our brains are what make us human. How we use them decides our destiny. As a character in Archibald Mac-Leish's play *The Secret of Freedom* says, "The only thing about a man that is a man, is his thinker. Everything else you can find in a pig or a horse."

Many years later, at the Stanford University Hospital, I remembered that line again when a team of surgeons skillfully replaced my tired aortic heart valve with one from a pig—a porcine valve. I'm delighted that my parts are interchangeable with those of our barnyard friends. All but one: my "thinker." And that's what makes me special. That's what makes you special. Our minds are the gyrocompasses of our lives. Once set, that's where we're going until they are reset.

I was amazed that I had not seen the answer before, but I was delighted nonetheless that I was at last in possession of the key. I had found the secret, although the fact that it was a secret to so many was strange indeed. Now, to make my living by writing my own radio programs demanded only that I resign a very good job with CBS and strike out on my own. I did both in March 1950, and I have been on an unbroken upward curve ever since. Those six simple words, in that order, revolutionized my life. I had found them, clearly spelled out, just as I had so desperately hoped as a child of twelve to find them, not in some hoary, ancient tome, but in a book published in 1937 entitled *Think and Grow Rich* by a man named Napoleon Hill.

Later, through my friendship with W. Clement Stone, a Chicago insurance tycoon, I met and got to know Napoleon Hill. I'll never forget our meeting. It took place at the old Edgewater Beach Hotel on Chicago's far North Side. I remember seeing this very thin, smiling old gentleman coming down a curving marble staircase. As he approached me, he held out his hand and said simply, "I'm Napoleon."

I recall fighting back the urge to respond with something like, "How do you do? I'm Alexander the Great." But this was the man who had managed to extract from the major philosophies and religions of the world, and the life stories of dozens of America's most successful people, the six words that explained better than any others why people live the lives they do.

Growth and increase and life abundant are the way of nature. It is inherent in each of us to desire more life and more of what life has to offer. That is not wrong. It is perfectly natural and the way it should be. The winners in the world are those men and women who plan it that way; they are people with a vision of the future that is sufficiently important to them that they are willing to do what is necessary to arrive in the midst of their vision.

As Theodosius Dobzhansky wrote in *Mankind Evolving:*

> Through his images of the future we come to know man, who he is and how he wishes to be; what his thoughts are, what he values most highly, what he thinks is worth striving for, and whether he thinks it is attainable. Certain types of men hold certain types of vision, subject to their temper and spirit. Tell me what your vision of the future is, and I will tell you what you are.

Perhaps now would be a good time to ask the question: "What is your vision of your future?"

When our thinking is chaotic, our lives are chaotic. Visualization is the human being's vehicle to the future—good, bad, or indifferent. It's strictly in our control. We must not make the mistake of falling into a lockstep to nowhere by assuming that the people whose lives are the pattern for our own know where they are going. Perhaps they think you are the leader. And perhaps, like processionary caterpillars placed on the rim of a flower pot, you are not going anywhere. So let's ask that question: "What is your vision of your future?"

We become what we think about. If you know what you want to become, you will become it. Visualization is a force of incalculable power. As Calcutta poet Rabindranath Tagore reminds us;

> Faith is the bird that
> Feels the light and sings
> When the dawn is still dark.

We grow into our expectations. It's too bad that so few manage to muster expectations that are in keeping with their true potential.

A business executive leaves his home to go to the office. It is early summer, a beautiful morning. He drives his late-model, expensive car, shining from frequent washings, out of the garage, sweeps down the drive to the shaded street, and turns toward town. On both sides of the street fine homes can be seen, their lawns and landscaping well cared for, their paint bright, their windows sparkling clean in the early morning light. Our business executive drinks in the sight. "Beautiful!" he says to himself. It's a lovely morning, all is well, and his world is in order. His fine car makes hardly a sound as it moves along the clean, orderly street. The neighborhood, and the homes up and down the street, reflect the people in his socioeconomic group. It's as natural for our business executive and his wife to have chosen the home in which they live and to pay the price for it as it is for any family anywhere. *They think and live in those terms.* The neighborhood reflects them, their education and aspirations, and their levels of accomplishment, and their way of life costs them no more from a percentage-of-income standpoint than do the homes and neighborhoods of anyone else in the country. And—this is important—once acquired, that home and neighborhood and society constantly reinforce their view of themselves and their place in the scheme of things. They may move farther upward or sideways, but the chances of their moving backward or downward are so small as to be negligible. Their environment is a mirror of their current place on the human achievement ladder.

At work, his office is also a reflection of him and a reinforcement of his place in the scheme of things. And when our executive drives home in the evening, he is bathed once more in the agreeable ambience of his place in the world. His world is a reinforcing mirror of his thoughts—a mirror of him, his wife, and his family. He is what he thinks about.

Not long ago I received a letter from a radio listener in Tarzana, California, Rabbi Steven Reuben. He enclosed copies of two sermons he had delivered to his congregation. One of them was entitled "You Already Know the Secret." In his letter to me he wrote: "This talk was inspired by your own messages, and I'm sure you will recognize many of the quotations that you have used in the past."

In his sermon, the rabbi said, "Yes, I did discover the secret of success, and it led me to explore the thoughts of authors, poets, philosophers, prophets, sages and a host of teachers of our time and ages past to discover what each of them believed about the secret of success.

"What I discovered was astounding. I found an abundance of wisdom as ancient as our 3,000-year-old Torah and as modern as twentieth-century science. To my amazement I realized that from the Bible to the Greek philosophers, from the wisdom of Rome through medieval studies of the human condition, from Shakespeare to Milton, to Emerson to the Rabbis of the Talmud, each had discovered an answer to the secret of success. But the most astounding discovery of all was the realization that *all of them*, each in his own language and in his own way, had discovered the exact same secret. This universal key to success simply put is this—'As you think, so shall you become.'"

> *Thought in the mind hath made us.*
> *What we are by thought was wrought and built.*
>
> James Allen
> "As a Man Thinketh"
>
> *We live in... thoughts, not breaths....*
> *He most lives who thinks most.*
>
> Philip Bailey
>
> *As he thinketh in his heart, so is he.*
>
> Proverbs 23:7

And how did Buddha put it? "As the wheel follows the ox behind, so we become what we think about." May his enlightenment forgive my Anglicizing.

Yet you can ask one hundred people in New York or Chicago or Los Angeles the question, "What is the secret of success?"—and they will look at you as if you're mad, or come up with a dozen clichés, or shake their heads and walk on. Not one of them will say, "The secret of success—or failure, for that matter—is that we become what we think about." They certainly didn't know about it in my old neighborhood in Long Beach, California, and they still don't. How can something so important remain a secret to so many? What could be more important to us than the answer to why we become what we become?

You are, at this moment, the sum total of all your thoughts up to this point in your life. And so am I. And so is that man across the street and that woman going into the supermarket. Watch them, study them, look at their faces. They are the most interesting creatures on the planet, and the most charged with possibilities. But do they know that? Do they know that their daily lives are mirrors of their thinking? Do they know about the subject we're discussing here? Alas, no. Most of them do not. Most of them are simply maintaining their position in the socioeconomic pyramid that they have unconsciously chosen as their lot in life. They do not know that by thinking in new directions (which has been called the definition of genius) they can bring new directions into their lives. Most of them are marking time, as if they have a noncancelable contract with life. How can we rise above our more egregious mistakes if we just mark time! Let's do it better than it's been done before. Let's find our partner in the freest, richest land on earth and do something wonderful with this holiday we've been mysteriously granted.

Here's where our individual and original DNA double helixes come into the picture. Each of us is an original, whether we like it or not. Each of us has a genetic profile unlike that of any other person who ever was or ever will be upon this planet. That is true because no one else in the universe has our particular set of ancestors or our exact genetic mix. Each of us might think of himself or herself as a painting. Each of our parents and each of our parents' thousands of ancestors has placed a daub of paint on that painting. After you were born, your environment began adding to the painting that is you. That composite work determines the way you tend to think. What you can do and what you want are different from what I can do and what I want and they are different in some ways from what everyone else can do and wants. That's what keeps everybody from wanting and doing the same thing.

Our rich genetic inheritance gives each of us a wide range of options, and our free society gives us free choice. The better the environment in which we are raised, and the better our education as young people, and the better the education of our parents, the greater the spectrum of possibilities to which we will be exposed during our formative years. But chosen at random, the odds are about ninety-five to five that that ideal background is not ours.

As for our mythical executive driving to work, as for people everywhere, an environment reflects the people who live there. Change the people through education, and the environment will change to reflect that degree of enlightenment, however slight, however great. I want you to consider your own environment from your earliest memories right up to the present time. By *environment* I mean the house you lived in as a child, the neighborhood, the family itself. What were the educational backgrounds .of your parents? The neighbors? Would you say your environment as a child was lower class, lower-middle class, upper-middle class, or upper class? Whatever it was, it had an enormous conditioning effect upon you. Perhaps it's a mold you would just as soon maintain, as would, perhaps, the children of our mythical executive and his wife. Those children will take the good life—the clean home environment, the good schools, the fine cars, the beautiful furnishings, the room of his or her own with all the sophisticated electronic gadgetry, the housekeeper, all of it—for granted. It will be as natural for them to live in such surroundings as it is for a poor child of the ghetto to live with dirt and disarray, with cold in the winter and stifling heat in summer, with undernourishment and lack of medical care, with going to the public school hungry in the morning. And for most in the United States, it's somewhere in between the two.

The children of our executive and his wife will take going to college for granted as a natural part of growing up, as will the children with whom they associate. For such children, survival and affluence are givens. Their concerns begin above that line. Their major problems concern the college or university for which they might qualify, or what to choose as a career after college. The ideas of success or failure are as foreign to them as the language of the Tierra del Fuegans. They are part of the successful minority; they belong to the top three percent of the American population and simply take it for granted. Not so, perhaps, for their parents, But for them succeeding is simply doing what comes naturally. And of course there's their inheritance, which will one day further bolster their place in the world—the family home, the family friends, the family world.

Someone once wrote: "If you suffer without succeeding, it's so that someone may succeed after you. If you succeed without suffering, it's because someone suffered for you. But there is no success without suffering."

I think the word *suffering* used in that context is meant to mean *striving*—making the grade to a new, higher level. In every family of affluence, someone somewhere had to climb from a lower level to a higher level. Even the British royal family had a poor striver somewhere in the past. *Old money* simply means that several generations have lived in the lap of luxury because some character back there had a good idea and worked his rear end off—and probably had a wonderful time doing it—to move the family from the poor neighborhood to the rich neighborhood. All old money was once *nouveau riche,* despite claims to the contrary. Once a fortune has momentum, it's not all that difficult to build it into a great fortune; there are experts who do nothing else and who would be delighted to do the same for you and me. It's getting it started that takes the unusual person, the person who simply refuses, for whatever reason, to march in lockstep with the big gang going nowhere, the person who does something of unusual value.

From the ship on which I was stationed in Hawaii, I used to watch the Navy PBY's—flying boats—take off from Pearl Harbor for their patrols. Sometimes the water would be so still, so smooth and slick, it would form a suction on the plane's hull, and even though the plane would have air speed, the hull would stick to the surface of the water. Then the pilot would rock the plane back and forth, and finally, on a backward tilt, the hull would break loose as a metaphor for breaking loose from debilitating traditions. It's difficult to be the one person out of many generations to break the mold and fly free and clear of the past. We see so many people we know and with whom we were raised who have not broken loose— our relatives, our closest friends. There is a strong tendency to remain in one's class, if I may use the word that was supposedly cast away when we emerged victorious as an independent, free nation.

We do have classes in America, whether we care to admit it or not. Our classes are not designed by artificial rank; we have no lords and ladies, no dukes, earls, or marquises, no princes, queens, or kings, but we have classes all the same. And in our society our classes are designated first by speech and education, second by money, and third by more money.

When a person opens his or her mouth and talks in the United States, he or she tells all within earshot the class in which he or she resides. There is uneducated speech and there is educated speech, and everybody knows the difference, except perhaps some of those in the uneducated-speech class. We may dress beautifully and drive up in a fine, expensive car, but if we get out and ask, "Where's the doorman at?" we have, with that simple, innocuous preposition, stripped ourselves to our underwear for any discerning person in the immediate area.

Like bad breath, the person with lower-class speech is usually completely unaware of his or her problem. But there will be a sizable and enjoyable world into which he or she will be forever barred from entering. It isn't snobbery; it's simply a matter of not fitting in. Poor speech cannot be hidden away; it's there, continually, as obvious as a cigar butt in the punch bowl.

Anyone can learn to speak the English language properly. It's difficult when one's parents, neighbors, brothers, sisters, and friends all murder the language, but it's still quite possible. It's a matter of education. It's a matter of paying attention in English class, no matter how poorly and uninterestingly it may be taught. There are excellent books on the subject, as well as tape cassette programs produced by my company. *

* Nightingale-Conant Corporation, 7300 North Lehigh Avenue, Chicago, IL 60648

If raping the English language were a misdemeanor, the people in my old Long Beach neighborhood, including the members of my family, would have been sentenced to death. Learning to speak and write our beautiful language—the world's largest and most interesting—does not require a special talent, like playing the clarinet or drawing. It's a matter of desire plus reading and study. There is no more important subject taught in school. In fact, it is the key to all the other subjects as well as to a whole world of interest and opportunity. It is the first step up to that higher, cleaner plateau where the air is fresher and the view much better. An hour a day of serious reading and study will handle the matter. And as you read, write. Copy long paragraphs so that you learn how words are properly strung together by accomplished writers.

While working on this book in our ninth-floor apartment in southwest Florida, my telephone rang. It was a substitute Federal Express woman wanting to get in the main door on the first floor. I was about to buzz her in when she asked, "Where are you at?"

"I'm on the ninth floor," I replied.

I waited at the front door of the apartment for her to get off the elevator, and when she did she repeated her earlier statement; "I didn't know where you were at."

Since she seemed to be in a happy frame of mind, I jokingly said, "Where did you learn that 'I didn't know where you were *at*' business?"

She said, "That's the way they talk in the part of Kentucky I'm from."

"That's no reason to go around a beautiful place like this trying to convince people that you're illiterate," I said.

"I'm not illiterate, Mr. Nightingale!" she said, and now it was no longer funny.

"Then why don't you stop trying to convince people that you are?" I asked, knowing full well that I had stung her. I didn't make a friend that morning. But I hope I converted her. She will no doubt be a mother someday. Not only will her speech have an important effect on whom she marries, and even on whether she marries, it will have a very serious effect on her children. That's the way ignorance gets passed along from one generation to another. It's that absurd old "What was good enough for Pappy is good enough for me!" balderdash—a ridiculous cop-out. What was good enough for Pappy is not good enough for anybody today. How can we advance as a species if we attempt to stand still? And if the person who says "What was good enough for Pappy is good enough for me" had to go back and live the life that Pappy lived, he would be a very disillusioned and unhappy man.

All that was required for my conscientious Federal Express woman was the question, "Where are you?" or "On what floor do you live?"

The book I most frequently recommend to those who care to brush up on their speech and writing is *The Elements of Style* by William Strunk, Jr., and the late E.B. White. It's a Macmillan paperback that will fit in your pocket or handbag. Another book you will enjoy very much and from which you will learn a great deal about good writing is *The Careful Writer* by the late Theodore M. Bernstein, published by Atheneum. A very good idea is to begin to build a collection of excellent books on English. Keep in mind that you can become an expert on anything in five years or less.

The most important thing I ever learned in my life is that we become what we think about. What do you think about? What is your goal? Can you write it out in a single sentence? One goal at a time, please. If you have more than one, or if you have some intermediate goals that lead toward a large goal, list them separately and number them 1, 2, 3, 4, and so on. Then answer this question:

You are today the sum total of your thoughts, up to this point in your life. Are you pleased with your present place in the world?

If your answer is yes, what's your next port of call?

If your answer is no, what are you going to do about it? What are you going to start thinking about? We control what we think about, and by so doing, each of us tells to an altogether unsuspected extent his or her own fortune.

I received a letter along with a little poem some time back from a radio listener. In her letter the woman wrote, "I have always wanted to write poetry." But I could tell from the note and from the poem that the woman was not really serious about writing poetry and, in fact, didn't know the first thing about the subject. The person who wants to write poetry and who is truly serious about it reads poetry, owns dozens of books of poetry, has studied writing and poetry, and has worked long hours at that difficult and demanding craft. She was much like the woman who gushed to the concert pianist following a concert, "I'd give anything to play as you do!" Which prompted the pianist to comment, "Except twenty years and seven hours a day."

Our world tells us the truth about ourselves. It reveals what we have learned, what we have done, and how much we have served. An old saying, "What you are speaks so loudly, I can't hear what you're saying," is apt. Don't tell me what you are going to do. Show me—go do it! I've always felt that glibness is a serious danger to accomplishment. Like a steam valve, if we talk at great length about what we are going to do, we seem to lose just that much steam when it actually comes to doing it. Another cliché puts it well: "Actions speak louder than words."

A couple traveling in India noticed a pleasant-appearing young Indian man sitting by a bridge near their hotel. They saw him sitting in that one spot day after day. Finally, becoming curious, they asked him why he sat there by the bridge all day, every day. He replied, "I happen to believe in reincarnation. I believe that I have lived many times before and that I will have many lives following this one. So this life I'm sitting out."

He had a plan and was engaged in following it. How about you?

On occasion I have been asked by serious people, "You say that we become what we think about. But what about people who choose dreams too large for their inherent capacities?"

Discounting serious neurosis or outright psychosis, it has been my experience that, far from choosing goals too great for our inherent capacities, we tend to underestimate ourselves and set them much too low, especially in the beginning. There seems to be a natural human tendency to take the accomplishments of others in stride but to doubt the accomplishments we ourselves can reach. We've lived in our own skin so long, we tend to take ourselves for granted; we tend to underestimate our potential for growth and achievement.

Remember that I am not encouraging you to reach for the moon, although that's already in the record books, too. What I'm suggesting is that you make an assessment of where you are and where you would like to be, establish a worthwhile goal, begin to think about it, and, as you do, realize that you become what you think about. Perhaps, like millions of others, you haven't been doing very much thinking at all. You may have just been part of the crowd, with your miraculous mind in neutral, waiting for you to give it a worthwhile job to do.

If you have difficulty deciding what you would most like to do, here's a little game you can play that might help you decide. Let's say you are financially independent. You have a very good income and don't have to concern yourself about it. It's Monday morning; you wake up feeling well, and you can do anything you want to do. What would you most enjoy doing? And what would you most enjoy doing on Tuesday and Wednesday and Thursday and Friday? Write it down.

"Oh, that couldn't be it," someone will say. "I'd most enjoy sailing and working around boats!"

If that's what you would most enjoy doing, and you know that from having done it a great deal, then there's your key. There's something in the boat business for you. And there are fifty thousand parts to the boat business, or any other business. It's a big industry, and if it's your thing, go to it.

Whatever your mind most naturally turns to, that's probably the key to an enjoyable and productive future. Examine it, write it down, explore it from every possible angle. There's opportunity there—worlds of it!

We do not seriously choose goals that are beyond our inherent capacity to achieve. Our very choice is determined by what we are—our genetic set, we might say. But in doing that which we most enjoy, we will probably make our most significant contribution to society. And the contribution we make to society determines our rewards.

CHAPTER II

A Place for Each of Us

As You Sow...

In doing that which we most enjoy, we will probably make our most significant contribution to society, and the contribution we make to society determines our rewards.

As you sow, so shall you reap.

The more one thinks about that great truth, the more one would like to see it emblazoned on the walls of schoolrooms, boardrooms, and government agencies, as well as in periodic television messages, in radio spots, and on appropriate outdoor advertising.

Anyone who has been an adult for an appreciable length of time can assess the extent and quality of his or her sowing by the simple expedient of taking inventory of his or her harvest. Our harvest at any point in our lives is the total input from our world; it is represented by our family, our spiritual life, the friends we have acquired, the attitude of our co-workers toward us, the place in which we live, the things we own, and, of course, our financial return. Our harvest, at any given time, is the total of what we have accumulated and are receiving from the world in which we are participating. And it is dependent on the extent and quality of our efforts and service. As we sow, so we reap—cause and effect. For every action there is an equal and opposite reaction.

You needn't bother to look for exceptions to that rule; there aren't any. The great law does not deviate for anyone. If your grandfather left you three hundred million dollars after taxes, you would still be subject to the great law of cause and effect: you would be happy or miserable or a combination of both, and you would be successful or unsuccessful as a person, depending solely on causes you set in motion. As *you* would sow, so would *you* reap, all the years of your life. If you sow friendship, you will receive friendship in return; if you sow love, you will receive love in return; if you sow that which is good and beneficial to all concerned, your harvest will be good and beneficial to you. But it is we who must set the law in motion; and in cases where the law has been set in motion by others, our response as a participant will keep it going or stop it dead in its tracks as far as we personally are concerned.

I have long used the metaphor of the woodstove. We must supply the wood and strike the match if we desire heat in return. To sit in front of a cold stove and demand that it supply heat first, before we take any action, is to sit in front of a cold stove forever. You might wonder how a person with many millions of dollars can be thought of as unsuccessful, but that can easily be the case. A person may be earning a very large return on his or her fortune as it works in productive investments; he or she may be financially secure, to say the very least. But that does not mean that the personal harvest exceeds the personal sowing. It cannot. Howard Hughes might be thought of as an extreme example. He was enormously rich, yet he lived in a prison of his own fashioning and suffered from malnutrition and personal social deprivation because of his psychotic attitude toward existence, the world, and the people in it. He was, in the end, a miserable failure as a human being, although his companies, under proper management, performed well and grew apace. Hughes himself reaped the most barren harvest possible; it matched perfectly his sowing.

So does your harvest and mine, and they always will. A "what's in it for me?" attitude preempts heat from the woodstove by not bothering to supply the wood and light the fire. People say, "I need a job," or, "I need work." Here once again we have the cold–stove metaphor, the childish acquisitiveness. How different it would be if the same people said, "I know I can be of service to the people of this community. Now, what can I do that will best serve these people and that I will still enjoy providing?" Here we have the wood and the striking match at least in inchoate form. We're on the right track.

Albert Einstein was once asked, "Doctor, why are we here?" He turned to his questioner in surprise that he had asked so elementary a question and replied, "We are here to serve other people." Of course! We are here to serve. Everything that we ever receive and from which we derive special pleasure and joy comes to us as a result of our having served. It's the key to a happy marriage and a happy family. It's the key to a happy organization of any kind.

The most joy we derive from occasions such as Christmas comes to us when others open their gifts from us. Things we can buy for ourselves, especially things we have long wanted, are a joy as well, but our buying them is a result of our service to others. That's where the money comes from. The amount of money we receive will always be in direct proportion to our service.

Here is the answer to the question that bothered me as a youngster: "Why do some people earn more money than others when they work about the same amount of time?" In fact, there is a small percentage of people whose earnings bear little or no relation to the time spent working. Why is that? It has to do with the nature of their service, coupled with the ancient law of supply and demand.

A man with the talent to pitch twenty or more winning baseball games or to bat over .300 is going to be paid great sums of money during the time he can perform such game-winning feats. That's because there are very few like him; every team wants him, and he can demand top dollar. He's a star. He entertains millions of fans (*entertains* means "serves") for many years and perhaps earns a place in the Hall of Fame. Andrew Lloyd Webber writes hit musicals. He wrote the *Cats* score and the music for *Joseph and the Amazing Technicolor Dreamcoat, Jesus Christ Superstar,* and *Evita.* So now he has a sixty-seven-acre Berkshire estate sporting a forty-room mansion, a Mayfair, London duplex, and more money than he knows what to do with. He has entertained (served) millions and will no doubt continue to do so as he makes his astonishing talent available to the world.

Turn what you have into something hundreds, thousands, or even millions of people can use and/or enjoy, and you may purchase fabulous personal things, too. As we sow, so shall we reap. If our sowing serves great numbers of people, our harvest will reflect that.

We could hold a convention of twenty-game-winning pitchers, .300 hitters, and writers of hit musicals in our living room. They are rare and valuable creatures indeed.

Every field of human endeavor has its stars; all the rest in those fields are in a descending order of what we might call the "service-reward" continuum. I once asked the price of a Joan Miro original in San Francisco and was told that it was $600,000. It does not hang in my home. But it no doubt hangs somewhere, and it's worth every penny of its price because there are only so many of them, and there is a ready market that will pay that kind of price for them. His was an astonishing talent.

What have you and I got to sell?

That's what it comes down to. What will the world pay for what you do at this stage of your life? You don't have to be a superstar to be a winner. There are a lot of very successful professional baseball players who earn excellent incomes in the pursuit of the career they love and who are not twenty-game-winning pitchers or .300 hitters. Just becoming a professional ballplayer puts one in a rather small and first-class community that is much admired and well paid. That in itself is success of a rare order; a similar situation exists in all fields.

How many people in the United States do what you do? And in the field in which you serve, where would you say you stand in its hierarchy of value? Not as a human being, but as one who serves others. Would you be near the top where the numbers grow smaller, or lower in the socioeconomic pyramid, where the numbers are greater, or somewhere in the middle?

That is why some people earn more money than others: they have made themselves more valuable as servers of others—more in demand.

Lower in the socioeconomic pile we find great numbers of people working in jobs that require little in the way of talent and training: baggage handlers, waitresses, cab drivers, clerks in stores, security guards, laborers. If one of these people should fall ill, he or she can easily be replaced. The person replacing him or her may not do the job nearly as well but can do the job nonetheless. Since there are so many people who can do that kind of work, the demand for such people, while vast, is easily filled and the pay is low. How difficult is he or she to replace? The answer results in a small paycheck.

Anyone willing to do that kind of work must be willing to accept that kind of pay. It's true that first-class waiters in first-class restaurants take home excellent pay. But they are paid only when they are working or are on paid time off, such as sick leave or paid vacations. They are in a personal service business. If they're not there personally, their income stops.

So is the dentist and the physician. When the dentist stops putting his hands into people's mouths, his income stops—at least, the portion of it that relies on his professional services; he may have investments that, working for him, provide him with a very good return. The same for the physician—he or she must be present physically in order to keep the income coming in. The same is true of many fields of endeavor.

But Andrew Lloyd Webber earns money every time one of his songs is played and every time one of his musicals is performed, whether he goes on working or not. Of course, his work is immensely enjoyable for him. Writing delightful music is difficult work, but for him it's also play. He loves to do it.

What do you love to do? What can you do that will earn you a lot of money even when you're playing golf or out on your boat? What do you love to do that can serve others without your having to be there personally? How can you beat the "personal service" requirement of so many jobs?

The twenty-game-winning pitcher has to appear on the mound for those games and for the games he can't win as well. But being a star, he can put away in good investments so much money during a ten-year career that he can then go fishing for the rest of his life if he so chooses. He served so many millions so well during a working career of ten years that he has it made. So does Marvelous Marvin Hagler and my good friend Famous Amos of chocolate-chip cookie fame who now spends most of his time in Hawaii.

If you love dentistry and its challenges, take care of your health and practice your profession as long as you can. You love what you do, and it keeps you happy and earns you an excellent living. If being a first-class waiter in a first-class restaurant brings you into daily contact with the friends you have made over the years and keeps you active and young and you love it, stay with it. Take good care of your feet and enjoy. Nothing is more satisfying than first-class people doing first-class jobs. We need all we can get, and we will pay them well. They are at the top of their professions, and God love them. I know I do.

It's the same with excellent gardeners—excellent people in all walks of service. We simply cannot find too many of them. They love their work, and it shows, and they will earn top dollar in their fields.

You can be in a personal line of service, or you can produce something that will make you wealthy or provide you with an excellent income whether you continue to work or not. The choice is yours. Yes, the choice *is* yours to make. That is your part of the bargain. You don't have to have the unique talent of a twenty-game-winning pitcher or a .300 hitter, or the special talent of an Andrew Lloyd Webber to become a millionaire. What is it that you do best? What do you most enjoy doing? Chances are, there's a yawning opportunity lurking in there somewhere. I found my specialty; now what's yours? That's your part of the bargain.

Your rewards, all the years of your life, will be in precise proportion to your service. You are here to serve others, just as they serve you. How can you maximize your service? How can you serve not only your regular customers but perhaps the people in your profession as well?

I recall the Sixties, when rebelling young people were shouting from the barricades that they wanted to "do their thing." I wanted to shout back that that is the purpose of education. The better educated we become, the better we are able to discover just what our "thing" is and then do it to the best of our ability and energy in the service of others. Only in that way will we know the joy of duty to ourselves and the world in which we find ourselves. Only in that way will we experience the maximum reward.

> *I slept and dreamt*
> *That life was joy.*
> *I woke and saw*
> *That life was duty.*
> *I acted, and behold!*
> *Duty was joy.*
> Rabindranath Tagore

That, my friend, is what it's all about.

The successful man or woman is the person who can say, "This is the goal I'm working toward. And this is the way I'm going to get there. And when I reach that goal, I'll have others by that time, and I'll use this same system—improved by then—to reach those goals as well."

Can you say that?

If not, you still have some in-depth thinking and self-examination to do. And don't despair, that kind of personal maturity comes to different people at different stages of their lives. Mozart knew what he had to do when he was eight years old, and the whole world has been enjoying what he did ever since. Mozart was a musical phenomenon, a rare genius. Einstein was just twenty-one and recuperating from a cold when he promulgated his first earthshaking breakthrough in physics. But Goethe was in his eighties when he completed *Faust*. Once you put the formula together for yourself, you'll do more and have more fun during the following five years than you probably experienced during your entire life up to that point. As the poet Tagore reminds us, "Duty is joy," when we're totally immersed in something that we enjoy doing and that does a first-class job of serving others. Quite often, people who first discover their true love in the service they were mysteriously designed to perform find themselves saying in surprise, "Do you mean that I get all this money for doing this? I'd do it for nothing!" That's when you know you are in the right line of endeavor. That's when you become, in your own way, a Walt Disney, a Henry Ford, one of the Wright Brothers, a twenty-game-winning pitcher, a .300 hitter, or a writer of one smash-hit musical after another.

It is my belief that there is a place in the overall scheme of things into which each of us will fit like a lost piece of a jigsaw puzzle if we will give the search for it the attention and time it deserves. That is our "journey into meaning"—the lifelong journey each of us is meant to take at birth.

But what about the ten zillion teenage girls who just want to get married and join the club? Sometimes they give one the impression that their combined intelligence would be hard-pressed to extricate the printed message from a fortune cookie. And those same ten zillion teenage girls will soon find themselves, if they don't manage to see a light brighter than the one they are presently following, near the bottom of the pyramid, there to remain for the better part of forty years, whether they get married or not. Crazy as it may seem, they actually want to belong to the big club, and they complicate their lives with marriage and children too soon, and then they spend the rest of their lives elbowing each other at the supermarket and living in housing developments.

They marry their male counterparts and then, as if magnetized, they stick to what Emerson called the great flywheel of society. That's why there are people who will clear your plumbing in Weed, California, or work on your septic tank in Gary, Indiana, or bag your groceries in Fort Myers, Florida. It's a beautiful system. No matter where you go, in this country or out of it, no matter how remote or inhospitable the place may seem to you, there will be people there filling all the necessary spots. There will be waitresses at the airport coffee shop, cab drivers, hotel clerks, bellmen at the town's main hostelry. And up and down every street in town, all the places will be filled with appropriate people doing their appropriate jobs to serve you. There will be unseen cooks at the Holiday Inn, and the gas stations will open on time.

So when you ask, "But what about the ten zillion teenagers who want to get married and join the big club?" there's your answer. *What in the world would we do without them?* Every one of them does exactly what you and I do: each one of them serves in his or her own way. It is a way that apparently meets their requirements; God bless them, we most certainly need them. When you see the young man walking out of the franchised restaurant in the morning wearing faded jeans, chewing on a toothpick, headed for his pickup truck and its waiting dog, remember that he's doing his part, somewhere; he's serving in his own way. Now, maybe he hasn't given the matter much thought, but his folks are proud of him, as is his young pregnant wife. He gets the job done.

During breakfast one morning in Monterey, California, an unusual event took place. I was reading the morning paper while waiting for my breakfast when a pretty young waitress suddenly ran past my table at high speed. As I watched her, she plumped herself onto her knees into the corner booth and began waving her arms frantically in front of the large window, her gaze fixed on something outside.

Looking down the hill to see what held her attention, I saw a young man on a bicycle crossing the intersection, heading away from us. Then he turned and looked up toward the restaurant. Seeing her in the window, he raised his left arm in recognition, then continued on his way.

The waitress watched him until he was out of sight. Then she turned to see a number of us watching her. She smiled ear to ear, blushing, her eyes brimming, and said to us, "That's my husband!"

It is rare to see such undiluted joy in a human being. Such love is heartening, indeed. And it made all of us who saw it aware that what we had witnessed was a very large and important part of life—the most joyous part. It's a phenomenon that transcends understanding. There's no defining it. When it happens, it's the greatest thing in the world, and why it happens, nobody knows for sure. There is a perfectly natural attraction between the sexes, to be sure. But there is nothing at all to equal the magical relationship that occasionally exists between one particular woman and one particular man.

Everyone who saw what happened in the restaurant that morning was cheered and warmed by it. Everyone was smiling and looking at the young woman. We were all happy for her.

Neither he nor she may think of what they do as serving others, but it is all the same. It keeps the whole shebang working. We'd be in a disastrous predicament if it were easy or common to pitch twenty winning games or bat .300 or write musical scores. Only three percent of the American working people earn $75,000 a year or more, according to the latest census figures. Out of more than 230,000,000 Americans, there are only about 800,000 millionaires.

The higher-income groups are small clubs, and the entrance requirements are demanding. You've got to render an uncommon service to earn $75,000 or more. And if you're up in the $250,000 range, you're meeting the needs or wants of a great many people, or you're selling something with a very large price tag to a select few. I imagine the sales commission on a Sperry Univac to the U.S. Air Force is considerable. One doesn't sell one of those every week or every month. But one way or another, the person in the rarefied upper income brackets is rendering an extraordinary service. She's not selling brassieres in Macy's.

Let me tell you how a friend of mine and his wife, working together, became millionaires. They began by rebuilding automobile engines. That is, Mervin, with a couple of helpers, was rebuilding automobile engines; Berryl took care of the growing family. But the deeply imbedded grease in Mervin's hands became a problem. They couldn't get them clean. So they began experimenting (trying to solve the problem) with different materials that would clean the deeply imbedded black grease and not destroy the hard-working pair of hands at the same time. They began experimenting with different kinds of cleaners and different kinds of creams for the protection of skin. And one day they put together a product that did the job. It actually cleaned the hands and kept them soft and comfortable. It worked beautifully for Mervin. And so they let a friend with the same problem try their concoction. It worked for him, too, and he and his wife raved about the product.

Mervin and Berryl called the product Flight and began selling it all over South Africa (that's where my friends live). They were wonderfully successful, although they had to come up with an entirely new way of distributing and selling their product. In each town in the country, they recruited young women to call on service stations and garages. Wherever people worked with dirty machinery, the young women would demonstrate the product and take orders. They were happy with their commissions, the customers were happy with the new product, and Berryl and Mervin, who were now mixing the stuff by the ton, were happy with their profits. They became so successful that a big cleansing-product company bought their company from them for five million rand (about five million American dollars). Mervin and Berryl deposited their newfound wealth and went about the business of raising their five children. But the big cleansing-product company was too institutionalized to bother with a sales force of young women that demanded personal attention and very special know–how; after two or three years, its directors gave the company back to Mervin and Berryl, saying they couldn't be bothered. So Mervin and Berryl got the five million rand and their company back. They are now in the process of marketing their product overseas.

Mervin and Berryl Nyland and their five fine children are among the nicest people we know. Becoming millionaires has only made them better. They started by rebuilding engines. Did you know that Wrigley's chewing gum was once a premium in a box of soap powder?

W. D. "Bo" Randall makes handmade knives of such quality, there's a four-year waiting list for them. Randall, a handsome man of seventy-three, began producing handmade knives in 1937 as a hobby but ended up the undisputed granddaddy of benchmade knife design. His fabulous handmade knives are of such quality that NASA included them in the Mercury astronauts' survival packs. You can see his beautiful products in the Smithsonian Institution and other museums. His knives are priced from $130 to $600 and more, and he can't meet the demand for them. The least expensive of his products takes at least twelve hours to produce by hand.

Does the young man in the faded jeans with the toothpick between his lips think about this as he leaves the restaurant and heads for his pickup truck? Probably not.

Do you think about things like this? Examine what you do every day. There are more opportunities presently lurking in your present work, regardless of what that work may be, than you could develop in a lifetime. If you're a janitor, can you make a better broom, or mop, or cleaning product? What do you see as you go about your work that could stand improvement? How can you multiply your services?

It is often the multiplication of what we do that is the key to increasing our service-rewards ratio. Once my radio program was heard on one radio station in the United States. As I write this, my daily commentary, *Our Changing World,* is heard on hundreds of radio stations throughout the United States, Canada, Mexico, Australia, New Zealand, Fiji, South Africa, the Bahamas, and dozens of other places. Now, instead of talking with the radio listeners in only one market area, I talk to them in more than a thousand. Can you syndicate what you do?

Some years ago the distinguished actor Carroll O'Connor told me about his and his wife Nancy's early days in New York City. Carroll and Nancy had been teachers, but Carroll wanted more than anything else to be an actor. He knew with every fiber of his being that acting was the right career for him. So Carroll and Nancy reached an agreement. In order for Carroll to get the parts he needed to build his reputation as an actor, he had to be home when the call to audition came for a part. So they agreed that Nancy would work and he would stay home when he wasn't making the rounds of the talent offices and producers. He told me how he used to turn his face to the wall and pretend to be asleep when Nancy got up and got ready to go to work on those cold, dreary early mornings in New York. He hated the situation, but he knew it was the only way.

Gradually, the calls came, and one of America's finest actors began demonstrating his talent. After a while, Nancy no longer needed to get up so early on those cold mornings in their little flat in New York. The last time I visited them in their beautiful home in Hollywood, Carroll was on top of the pile, where he belonged and would remain, and Nancy was volunteering her talents for UNICEF in Los Angeles. A great team. It wouldn't have worked without the great partnership. In fact, we were together in Rome when Carroll told me about the new show Norman Lear wanted him to consider. It was called *All in the Family,* and it became the top-rated television series in the United States.

Years later, at a dinner with Carroll, Nancy, and Norman Lear in Hollywood, Lear told me that Carroll O'Connor was the only actor in the world who could have handled the Archie Bunker character in so endearing, outrageous, and hilarious a manner. He made millions forget their problems and laugh at silly and absurd prejudices. He became a living caricature of all that is stupid in our society—and we loved him for it. How well he served us was proved by the ratings the show received year after year. The entire cast was superb; Carroll O'Connor was brilliant!

We are served by thousands of unseen men and women every day of our lives. They pick the beans to make the coffee we drink; they harvest the wheat and bake the bread we eat; they milk the cows and process the milk we drink and the cheese we eat. They provide us with electricity and hot and cold running water; they heat our homes and produce everything that's in them, from the light bulbs to the carpeting, the glass, the wood, the steel, the concrete. They make the clothes we wear and the furnishings with which we daily live and the bedclothes and the thousands of little things we want and enjoy but don't really need. They manufacture our automobiles and process the gasoline and oil that powers and lubricates them. They do everything for us—*except decide what we do for them.* That is left to us. And making that decision, we determine our place in the scheme of things.

I read the other day about a twenty-nine-year-old woman entrepreneur who has three hundred cookie stores and is moving into Great Britain with them. If what you do warrants one store, how about a store in a thousand towns and cities?

Take what you do, what you most enjoy doing, and find a way to multiply it. You needn't hurry; slow, steady growth is best.

If you work at a salaried job, what is it about your work—some facet of your work—that can be developed into a multiplied service? What do you know that others need and want to know?

What's your hobby? Think—but think with a pen and a pad of paper. Keep paper and pen with you or near you at all times. You will want to start writing down your ideas.

Remember, your rewards must always be in proportion to your service. Find ways—good, solid, healthy ways—to increase your service, and your increased rewards will take care of themselves.

What percentage of people, do you think, have this service-reward idea straight in their minds? Would you say one percent? That would be a generous estimate. Yet how many people are familiar with the biblical statement, "As ye sow, so shall ye reap"? Ninety-five percent? About that. How many people believe it's literally true in our lives that it is more, much more than a happy saying from the Bible? That's right, they don't think about it in those terms. But the unbreakable law it describes is at work every moment of every day of our lives. Cause and effect. For every action there is an equal and opposite reaction.

Drive through the different neighborhoods in your town or city. Look at the homes and places of business. They mirror the people who live and work in them. Want to see a businessman or woman up close? Look at his or her place of business. Check the restrooms. You're looking at him or her. You may be seeing that person more clearly than he or she sees himself or herself. Look at the homes, the front yards. You're looking at the people who live there. They are telling you what they are doing for the community by displaying what the community is doing for them.

Drive by your own home. Better yet, pull up and stop. Take a good, long look. That's you and your family. We can most certainly change and, as we change, our world will change to reflect the changing and emerging being.

I recall reading that when Dr. Robert M. Hutchins, then chancellor of the University of Chicago, was told, "You can't teach old dogs new tricks," he replied, "Human beings are not dogs, and education is not a bag of tricks."

People can and do change. Our corporate files are bulging with letters from people who have written us about how they have changed as a result of information they obtained through our company. We've been getting letters like that for thirty years. Dr. Hutchins was right—people are not dogs, and education is not a bag of tricks.

The people have everything you and I might possibly want, and they will happily share it with us if we will qualify first by being of service to them—by providing them with something for which they will happily pay.

"He worked hard all his life, but he never had anything to show for it." Have you ever heard that comment? I have. As a youngster I heard it often. "He" apparently achieved a kind of parity between what he was doing for a living and the living it was paying for. His service was limited, and it limited his income. It apparently satisfied him; he did nothing to change it. Our housekeeper once commented that her husband couldn't understand why, no matter how hard he worked, he couldn't get ahead financially. It turned out that he was a mechanic; he worked on one car at a time for eight hours a day. How much can such work be worth? How much can each customer be charged? Then there's the overhead, the cost of doing business. By the time the mechanic is paid, it's true, it was going to be very difficult for him to get ahead financially. *But he chose that line of work.* And think of the things he chose not to do before he went to work as a mechanic. He chose to drop out of school. He chose not to work out a plan that would result in his owning his own business (not that that means he would have gotten ahead financially necessarily). He chose to take the path of least resistance every step of the way and is apparently quite willing now to work as a mechanic.

Mervin Nyland was a mechanic, too. He rebuilt engines, remember? And then he began experimenting with ways to keep his hands both clean and in good shape physically.

Both our housekeeper's husband and Mervin Nyland reap the harvest their sowing produces. One is poor; the other is a millionaire.

I remember an old poem I read as a youngster gobbling up books looking for answers. It began:

I bargained with life for a penny
And life would pay no more.

I don't remember the rest, but that's not important. What's important is that life will pay us what we bargain for, and if we play for peanuts, we're going to have to eat peanuts.

How can I multiply my service? How can I multiply my service to those I have chosen of my own free will to serve? That's my task, my responsibility.

But I must remember that my rewards, all the years of my life, will be in exact proportion to my service. If my service is sharply limited, my income will be sharply limited. If I can expand and multiply my service, my harvest will be multiplied accordingly. Service-reward—that's the way it works. We can work with the system or against it. But it remains the same. And it's beautiful when we begin to work with it. It's limitless, really. We're the limiters; we're the governors on the system. If it's held back, we do the holding. Look what it's doing for IBM! Even the American automobile manufacturers are beginning to figure it out: Give the people what they want, give them a quality product, and they'll buy from you.

People have needs and they have wants.

Their needs are few; their wants are limitless. Give them what they need or want, and they will reward you accordingly. Fail to give them what they need or want, and they'll put you out of business. Service-reward. No exceptions.

CHAPTER III

A River or a Goal

There are two categories of very successful people: those I call "River People" and those that might be labeled "Goal People." River People are those fortunate few who find themselves born to perform a specific task. They are usually well aware of just what that task is while they are still quite young. They are not interested in doing anything else. They are born to spend their lives in great rivers of the most absorbing interest, and they throw themselves into those rivers wholly. Mozart and Leonardo da Vinci were River People. There are hundreds of thousands of River People living today, and they can be found in all fields. They are our finest musicians and performers in all the arts; they are writers, scientists, and lawmakers and can be found in every profession.

Dr. Al Rhoton, a brilliant microneurosurgeon at the University of Florida, comes to mind as I write on this subject. He heads the Teaching Center and performs brilliant, life-saving surgical procedures. I saw a dozen or so physicians from all over the world at the Center, sitting in a circle, peering through powerful microscopes and operating on the brains of mice in order to perfect their skills in microneurosurgery. They use instruments specially designed for such fine work: tiny, delicate forceps; sutures so fine they're nearly invisible to the naked eye; and miniature scalpels. Their movements are barely perceptible as they work on nerves and tiny blood vessels.

Dr. Rhoton can be seen in the halls of the hospital from early in the morning until very late at night. One sunny afternoon we were taking a walk, and I asked him why he didn't have a high-priced practice in New York or Beverly Hills. He walked along in silence for a few minutes, then he said, "Where I get my satisfaction out of all this, Earl, is knowing that somewhere in the world, every day, people are getting better medicine, better surgery, because of what we're doing here." His work is his life, and vice versa. I'm afraid his family has not seen too much of him over the years; that's true of all River People.

Henry Royce was such a person. His obsession was to build the world's finest and quietest motorcar. Early in the twentieth century, when he started work on what was to become the world's standard for excellence in automotive design and manufacture, the automobile engine sounded like a modern clothes dryer filled with empty cans, punctuated with gunshots. Royce was convinced that the parts of an internal combustion engine could be finely manufactured to such exacting tolerances and so perfectly lubricated that the noise of their operation would be, or could be, barely perceptible to people standing nearby. He stalked about his auto plant in a nearly constant march. He would not take the time to eat; a boy was hired to follow him about with a sandwich and a glass of milk. When Royce became sleepy, he would lie on a cot in the plant and take a nap. Then he was up again, examining everything.

One day he overheard one of his engineers saying to a workman, "That's good enough," and Royce hit the ceiling. "It is not good enough!" he shouted. "It is never good enough. We strive for perfection. Since that's impossible, it's never good enough. Find a way to make it better."

I once toured the Rolls-Royce plant in London and was astonished at the care taken with imperfections that were invisible to me. Such care and dedication stood England in good stead during the Battle of Britain, when Rolls-Royce turned out engines for Spitfire fighters. A stained–glass window over the entrance to the company's headquarters was given to the company by a grateful nation.

Royce's unrelenting dedication is typical of the River Person; the great products and services of the world are usually due to such a person. Henry Ford accepted the challenge, which was at the time thought to be impossible, to produce a motorcar for the working classes. Henry Ford did not invent the assembly line—Eli

Whitney had done that with the manufacture of rifles—but Ford was the first to apply the system to the manufacture of automobiles. His genius for finding ways to cut costs and still produce a quality product was legendary. He raised the salaries of workers to a mind-boggling five dollars a day—a level never before equaled in the history of the Industrial Revolution. One of Ford's problems was that once he came up with a revolutionary idea, he was irrevocably fixed on it. The passage of time and changing economic conditions could not bring about changes in his way of thinking. But Henry Ford was a River Person. I'm sure you can think of many others. Perhaps you are a River Person.

Things aren't as simple and clear-cut as they once were. There's such a welter of possibilities—so many options—that it can be difficult for a person to find his or her main interest in life. If we haven't found the work for which we're best fitted, there is usually an unresolved feeling of discontent with what we are doing. If we were true to ourselves, we would say, "I know this work is not the work for which I'm designed," and begin to explore, in our spare time, other lines of endeavor. Too often we are guided more by the pay scale than by a genuine feeling of interest in the work itself. Whatever our true line of work turns out to be, with the kind of one-hundred-percent dedication and commitment we would give to it, it could produce everything we could possibly want.

My late partner, Lloyd Conant, was a River Person as far as our company and the kind of work we do were concerned. It seemed to fill his life completely. When he was not putting in long hours at his office or out at the plant, he was thinking about it or going over the books. From the day we formed the corporation by merging our two small companies in 1959, he was one hundred percent committed and thought of little else. We used to get together for barbecues in the Conants' backyard in Evanston, Illinois; even there the conversation would always seem to migrate back to the company, what we were doing, and what our plans were for the future. When he fell ill with the cancer that ended his life, he still worked at his office as long as he could, then worked at home still longer. Even when he was in the hospital, in severe pain and discomfort, the business was uppermost in his mind. It was his life, and he gave it the best that was in him to give.

Audio publishing did not exist as a business before we started our company. It can still be necessary, as it was for Steve Wozniak and Steve Jobs of Apple Computers, to have to start something new. Our company began with my writing and recording *The Strangest Secret*. Perhaps there's some pioneering work for you to do, too.

The old motion pictures keep coming back on cable television. Recently I caught a glimpse of a film that starred Mickey Rooney when he was a boy of perhaps thirteen or fourteen. Even before that, he had been a seasoned vaudeville and motion–picture veteran. He was a natural, as they say. He took to show business the way Mozart took to music or Edison to tinkering or Lindbergh to flying. Today, Mr. Rooney is a distinguished actor with an ability to do comedy, tragedy, or musicals with equal facility. He has been a show–business phenomenon since childhood. Success is something Mr. Rooney didn't have to worry about. He has a great, deep river of interest that has entertained millions and will go on entertaining millions for many years to come.

Walt Disney was another good example of a River Person; so were Birdseye of frozen food and Hershey of chocolate. River People are perhaps the world's most fortunate people; they identify the star they are meant to follow, and they follow it all their lives.

Each of us should watch for early, telltale signs of consistent and unusual interest, for the magnet in the midst of the spectrum of options that draws us toward itself as light is drawn toward a black hole. On rainy days, when we were children, out of school, what did we most enjoy doing?

Dr. Maslow has pointed out that in the best instances, the person and the job fit together like a key and a lock, or perhaps resonate together like a sung note that sets a particular string in a piano into sympathetic resonance.

He also said, "I have found it most useful for myself to differentiate between the realm of being (B-realm) and the realm of deficiencies (D-realm)—that is, between the eternal and the practical. Simply as a matter of the strategy and tactics of living well and fully and of choosing one's life instead of having it determined for us, this is a help. It is so easy to forget ultimates in the rush and hurry of daily life, especially for young people. So often we are merely responders, so to speak, simply reacting to stimuli, to rewards and punishments, to emergencies, to pains and fears, to demands of other people, to superficialities. It takes a specific, conscious effort, at least at first, to turn one's attention to intrinsic things and values—perhaps seeking actual physical aloneness, perhaps exposing oneself to great music, to good people, to natural beauty, and so on. Only after practice do these strategies become easy and automatic so that one can be living in the B-realm."

I believe that each of us, because of the way our genetic heritage is stacked, has an area of great interest. And it is that area that we should explore with the patience and assiduity of a paleontologist on an important dig. For it is a region of great potential. Somewhere within it we can find an avenue of interest that so perfectly matches our natural abilities that we will be able to make our greatest contribution and spend our lives in work we thoroughly enjoy.

Sir William Osler, the great physician, was a River Person. He was speaking to other possible River People when he said;

> Throw away, in the first place, all ambition beyond that of doing the day's work well. Find your way into work in which there is an enjoyment of it and all shadows of annoyance seem to flee away. Let each day's work absorb your energy and satisfy your wildest ambition. Success in the long run depends on endurance and perseverance. All things come to him who has learned to labor and wait, whose talents develop in the still and quiet years of unselfish work.

If you find yourself saying, "I must not be a River Person," wait. Think about it. Examine your life, your wants, your dreams, your daydreams, your visions. And look for a consistent key, a way in which you like to see yourself doing some particular thing as a form of work or service. A consistent daydream is often our inner intelligence trying to tell us what we should be doing. It may be that you are already in the general area you want to be in but just haven't seen its true possibilities. Discontented actors have found their Rivers in directing; discontented salespeople in sales management; and so on. Every industry has within it hundreds, if not thousands, of possibilities. There is advertising and art, public relations, purchasing—the list goes on and on. But keep this in mind: If it's the right work for you, chances are you've found yourself fooling around with it in your spare time in some way, or reading about it, or doodling about it, or visiting it in your free time. Look for a consistent interest. If you find it, you may have found your River. A River in carpentry is just as richly satisfying and fraught with possibilities as any other calling.

A friend of mine, Jim Hansburger of Atlanta, is an investment banker with Shearson–American Express. He's still a young man, yet he earns a million dollars a year or more in commissions. When he's not working with his clients, he's delivering lectures on business and sales. The last time I called him, he was at the University of Georgia teaching a class. He starts early and works late; he loves his work, and he fits the profession of investment banking the way a top-earning jockey fits thoroughbreds. Jim Hansburger found his River.

If we cannot find a special interest in a particular line of work, then we no doubt should become Goal People. There are those of us who seem to be able to do many things with equal facility and equal interest and enjoyment. There are, for example, professional business executives who simply love the challenge of business. They can take an ailing company and within a few years raise it to a level among the leaders. The company's product or service doesn't seem to make very much difference.

Lee Iacocca was known as an "automobile man" because of his many successful years at the Ford Motor Company. As such, he was asked to take over the Chrysler Corporation when it was in danger of complete collapse. That he did in a masterful, skillful way. That he risked his professional reputation in the process was an indication of his confidence. The rest of the story is history. But Lee Iacocca might have done just as well taking over a corporation that manufactured toys, copiers, computers, or whatever. Iacocca is a consummate American business executive; he revels in a challenge and in the resulting success and all that goes with it—the big money, the publicity, even the opportunity to run for President of the United States. Iacocca is a Goal Person.

Many will ask, "Why set goals at all? Why not just take things as they come and do your best with what you have 'been given' to do?" That "been given" business is often a way of saying you stumbled into a chance opportunity for work and simply stayed there.

A goal gives a picture to the human subconscious. Everyone has goals, whether he or she will admit it or not. Whatever you want to bring about in your life is a goal: that dress in I. Magnin's window, that sports car, that condominium apartment in Florida, that home in Martha's Vineyard, that man or woman you want to date. Wants are goals. But it seems that for most people, wants seldom get focused sufficiently or get mixed with enough positive expectation. "I want a lot of things," someone will say.

Without a goal we are much like the man with a boat and nowhere to go. Goals give us the drive and energy we need to remain on the track long enough for their accomplishment. Like the captain of the ship about to leave port, we should be able to tell anyone our next port of call, and perhaps the one after that, too. If you have done much traveling at sea, perhaps you were surprised at first by how slowly the ship moved through the water. In a time when it's common for us to drive at sixty and seventy miles per hour and eat lunch while tearing through the sky at six hundred miles per hour, a ship pulling away from a dock and heading for a distant port at twenty knots may seem painfully slow indeed. But the ship moves steadily, twenty-four hours a day, always on course, and the cumulative effect of such relentless singleness of purpose delivers us to the next port of call in a surprisingly short time. One day we raise the distant shore, and soon we're in the harbor, mission accomplished. Now, after refueling perhaps, and the scheduled stop, a new port of call must be determined.

People with goals on which they have set their hearts and minds are always moving toward those goals. Even while we sleep, our deep minds are working on the project. That's why we often awaken, early in the morning, with the solution to a problem that had repeatedly resisted our conscious attempts to solve it the day before. We think about our goal as we have our morning coffee and breakfast, while we're in the shower, and it comes to us again and again during the day. We are on course; we are moving toward the fulfillment of our current goal. And it is often the last thing we think about as we drop off to sleep. It is our aiming point. And people with aiming points tend to reach them.

It's interesting—and often quite astonishing—that people with goals tend to live longer than people without them. It's as if they can extend their lives simply because they have something to do. It must be the interest that lends vitality and energy to their lives.

There are fine old ships, beautifully maintained, still safely sailing the world's seas. They have successfully visited thousands of ports of call. There have been storms at sea and occasional breakdowns of one kind or another, delays when they have had to anchor offshore for a while. But the life of each of these ships has been one of one success after another. That's the way goal-oriented people spend their lives. Each goal, successfully reached, finds them better equipped, with more experience, to set the next goal. Goals for such people tend to ascend in stairlike fashion, each one a bit more demanding and fulfilling than the one before. In a few years they find themselves accomplishing, with surprising ease, goals that would have been impossible for them when they first began their journey into meaning.

Cervantes wrote; "The journey is better than the Inn." It's good to rest at the inn after a long journey, just as it's good for our ship to tie up at a dock for a few days' rest after a long sea voyage. But Cervantes was certainly right—the journey is better than the inn. The journey is life and experience; it puts us in the way of new interests and the most astonishing synchronicity. When a person knows where he or she is going and is engaged in getting there, the most amazing coincidences begin to take place. It's like reading something by Victor Hugo—the coincidences often take on the most outrageous appropriateness. Just as we're stumped, that one person with the answers happens along, or someone sends us the one book that has exactly the answer we were looking for. When we know where we're going and are occupied on our journey, it seems as if all the forces, whatever they are, come to our aid. We are helped along by invisible as well as visible sources. This is not to say that we encounter only smooth sailing; on the contrary, there will be a door like that of an exclusive club with a "Members Only" sign on it. It seems to exist to prevent all but the hundred-percenters from gaining entrance. Perseverance—dogged, unflagging, repeatedly rejected perseverance—is the answer, of course, and when we've set our heart and mind on something that is so important to us, we can generate that kind of persistence.

Quite often, if we read a story with the kind of coincidences that are often a part of a goal-oriented person's life, we would put it down, muttering, "Impossible!" But astonishing as it may seem, and astonishing as it sometimes seems to those of us in pursuit of a goal, that kind of synchronicity becomes an active part of the goal-oriented person's life. I say synchronicity rather than coincidence because I believe it is more than coincidence. It is a meshing, a coalescing of the parts necessary to the successful achievement of our goal. Sometimes it is baffling indeed and often leads us in a circuitous journey. A minor accident, or what appears to be a significant setback, turns out to be necessary if we're to get back on the right track.

But as Emerson wrote, "Trust thyself! Every heart vibrates to that iron string." We should learn to stay on the alert for serendipitous occurrences, accept them, and realize they are a part of the journey toward a goal—another reason why the road is better than the inn. We should not attempt to force such things; we must learn, as the Taoist reminds us, not to push the river. Stay on course, but go with the flow; the right things will happen at the right time, without forcing, without impatience. And we will find ourselves with our goal realized one fine day just as we'll raise the coastline of the port toward which our ship is churning, or our sailboat sailing. There it is! And we shield our eyes from the early sun and stand at the rail and imagine we can smell the land and hear the sounds of the busy harbor. Soon we're tied up at the pier, our latest journey a success. Now it's time to relax, enjoy the achievement, rest for a while.

I'm a golf fan, and I've always enjoyed watching the way the great players address and hit the ball. I haven't noticed him doing it lately, but in the days when he was breaking all the records, Jack Nicklaus had a most interesting style. He would take his stance at the ball and look at the spot on the fairway or the green where he wanted his ball to land. Then he would look at a point some six to ten feet in front of his ball, then at the ball—then at the point six to ten feet away, then at the point again on the fairway or green. He always seemed to have an intermediate point over which he wanted the ball to pass: he always had *two* aiming points—one quite close, the other where he wanted his ball to land. When he was ready, and not a moment before, he would uncork that legendary swing of his that left the gallery gasping and whooping with admiration and amazement.

Intermediate aiming points are often important to identify and establish on the way to any sort of really substantial goal. We know what our ultimate landing site is; we have established that— but where do we begin? That's where intermediate goals come into the picture. Quite often it is these intermediate goals on which people are reluctant to spend enough time. These are often the core skills vital to the completion of the final project. Here we find the person who wants to amaze friends with his or her skill at the piano but doesn't want to put in the time and effort required to learn to play well. This is the person who is forever looking for shortcuts. This person is a great daydreamer—but when it comes down to the nitty-gritty of the intermediate goals, ah, that's too difficult or boring or time-consuming. There are millions of fat people looking for a twelve-day miracle that will magically restore them to their perfect weight. But suggest they follow a regimen or learn new habits that will take off a pound a week for a year and at the same time cause them to put together a new lifestyle that will keep them trim for the rest of their lives—it's no deal. They don't want to change their eating habits; they only want to change their weight and appearance. So they remain fat.

Want to be a writer? How about spending some time studying the English language? How about reading some really good books? Spend a couple of years putting some real quality into your education!

Want to get rich in real estate? Learn the business first. The first step of the successful Goal Person is commitment. The person who is one hundred percent committed to the achievement of a goal is quite willing to take whatever intermediate steps are necessary. The bridges are burned; there is no escape route on

which to come tiptoeing back when things get rough. Commitment, one hundred percent.

When that happens, the goal is as good as accomplished, and
you'll have fun and great experiences on the road to its achievement. In fact, the goal itself may come as an anticlimax, demanding the immediate setting of a new goal. People who know such
committed persons and are privy to their goals also know that they
will reach those goals. They become silent and affirmative partners
and often set in motion events that will help along the way.

As we work to bring a difficult long-range goal to reality, we
gradually grow into the kind of people for whom such goals are
natural. That's because before we can do something, we must be
something. And to me, this way we have of growing to fit the work,
the social situation involved, the embodiment of superior achievement, are mind-boggling wonders. We actually *become* what we
think about. And the key to it all is that each of us must do the
thinking; each of us has his or her own governor tied to his or her
own innate capabilities. I could no more do the things Lee Iacocca
does than the pelicans that fly past my balcony every afternoon
could fly backward. I don't set the same goals Iacocca sets.

I cannot set your goals any more than you can set mine. You
are the only person alive who can set your goals, although others
may inspire you from time to time to do more than you might have
done without their encouragement. Encouragement is the function
of a good leader, a coach or manager. The presence of an inspired
and dedicated leader can significantly upgrade the performance of a
large corporation employing thousands of men and women. Hence
the saying that the success or failure of any organization is but the
lengthened shadow of its leader.

But the point I want to make here is that we all have basic and
inherent genetic differences. I knew a corporal in the Marine
Corps during World War II who could perform the most astonishing
tricks with his mind. Whenever some kind of test was ordered, he
easily outscored everyone else on the base, if not in the entire
corps. Both his mother and father were full professors at leading
universities. He came from a long line of people with high IQs and
as a result could think rings around most of the rest of us and do
mathematical problems in his head that we couldn't have done

under any circumstances. He had inherited a sixteen-cylinder brain. Our species needs such people for the special tasks they perform. There are also a lot of eight-, and six-, and four-cylinder brains, and we need those, too. And the most fascinating point of all this is that regardless of the genetic equipment we've been handed, the goals we set—and invariably reach when they are truly our goals and not the goals of a parent or acquaintance—meet our desires perfectly. We are quite happy with them.

The house and neighborhood that represent complete success and total satisfaction to one person might represent failure to another; they also might be the kind of home and grounds that most people are quite content simply to drive past with exclamations of wonder and delight.

That's why I have stressed that you examine your daydreams for signs of a repetitive picture. It may be the aiming point for the present. Just as coughing is the only way the lungs can beg a smoker to stop destroying them, our daydreams or habitual visions are often the way our inherent genetic mix is put together; those dreams and visions are trying to tell us which way to go. They are often the projection of our inner voice. And that inner voice is based on very sound judgment about our true inherent capacities.

One thing we must put aside in order to fulfill our unique possibilities is conformity. We all conform in hundreds of ways. Even those of us who feel we have gone our own individual ways in the world, who have lived more or less as free and independent spirits, are conformists to an extent that would surprise us if those ways were listed and printed out for us. But we need to recognize that there are ways in which we must not conform. And we need to recognize the fact that the tendency to conform to the standards of others without question is insidious and ever-present. There is a human tendency, no doubt acquired and strengthened in child-hood, to believe that whatever people in significant numbers are doing must be correct or so many of them wouldn't be doing it. That statement may never be spoken or thought in just that way, but I'm sure you know what I mean. When I was a youngster, popular things were believed to be best. Florsheim shoes were thought to be the best, as were Hart, Shaffner, and Marx suits—not that I ever owned either during that time. My father and no doubt hundreds of thousands in similar situations felt that Pontiac was the best car—but earlier it had been Buick, and before that, a Reo Flying Cloud. There were popular fads, and unless one conformed to them, one simply wasn't "in," or later, "hip." To flash the proper label indicated that you were knowledgeable about what to wear and drive.

The fact is, they were all wrong. The popular, heavily advertised brands were fine and suited the great masses of people quite handily, but they really were not the best that money could buy. The great majority of people seldom enjoy the best of anything. They don't drink the best Scotch or bourbon, wear the best clothes or shoes, or drive the best cars. The best is never the most popular.

I mention these things to establish the importance of questioning the things we do. Do we do them because they are what "everybody else is doing" or because we have come to the conclusion that they are best for us and our personal journey into meaning?

To young people the need to belong is paramount. The group is the thing, and to be a member of the group is quite sufficient—so sufficient that one is willing to lose every vestige of individuality and take on the trappings, speech, and habits of the group. "Oh, God, just let me belong!" is the unspoken prayer. And that's fine. It's their first true identity outside their families, and it's important. That it takes them far afield of what their parents traditionally expected is better yet. Outraging or at least amazing their parents is an important part of the act. And of course it is an act. Just as the thousands of college students on spring break who inundate the Fort Lauderdale, Florida waterfront are expressing their break with the polite routine of the family and their younger days. They are expressing their freedom from the family and from all other rules of human conduct by joining another group. They are still as individually faceless as they were before, perhaps more so, they are like a herd of white-faced Herefords, virtually indistinguishable from one another. But this passage rite is important to them. Fine. But after it, each of them must find his or her own pathway in the world; however, it is my observation that very few of them do. They simply leave one group to join another, and although they will soon put aside childish and primitive activities (defecating in dresser drawers and otherwise destroying and vandalizing the property of others is typical), chances are they will still represent a group and will act in unison in most ways. They will tend to live in tract homes or condominium apartments with all the charm and creative touches of an army barracks, and they will spend their entire lives taking their cues from their peer group. Reisman called it "other-directed," as opposed to "inner-directed," behavior. Until we begin living as inner-directed persons, we follow others who are, in turn, following us. Maybe there isn't a leader up there somewhere at all but rather just a huge circle with everybody following everybody else.

Although there are possibly exceptions—I have never found one—a good rule to follow is:

> Whatever the majority of people is doing, under any given circumstance, if you do the exact opposite, you will probably never make another mistake as long as you live.

You can apply it to education, driving your car, obtaining a job, or waiting until you find the woman or man who will be your companion for the rest of your life.

You and I are going to make a lot of mistakes along the way. One of the worst mistakes will be to get in our own way, that is, to override our real intelligence with expediency and the desire to conform with the rest of the people. If you do it with your golf swing, you get a ruined shot—not too bad, although a frustrating disappointment. If you do it while driving your car, it can kill you or someone else. And if you do it enough with your daily life—forget it.

We need to calm down, relax more, smile more. Pick that spot on the fairway or on the green where you want that lovely little ball to land, and then when you're ready, hit the ball.

River Person or Goal Person, and sometimes a combination of both, is the way to go. In the words of Robert Schuller; "God's word for today: find the gift that is in you."

CHAPTER IV

The Greatest Things on Earth

Man's greatness lies in the power of thought.
Blaise Pascal
1623–62

*Men fear thought as they fear nothing else on
earth—more than ruin—more than death. . . .*

*Thought is subversive and revolutionary,
destructive and terrible, thought is merciless to
privilege, established institutions, and
comfortable habit. Thought looks into the pit of
hell and is not afraid. Thought is great and swift
and free, the light of the world, and the chief
glory of man.*
Bertrand Russell,
mathematician-philosopher,
Nobel laureate

All of the above is true. A single thought can revolutionize
your life, as it did mine. A single thought can make you rich or
well-to-do, or it can land you in prison for the rest of your life.
Thoughts can be terrible or sweet and beautiful—it all depends on
the person doing the thinking. Ideas are the greatest things on
earth. The United States of America was only an idea until acted
upon. Everything was an idea before it became real in the world.

55

Your life is the result of your thoughts; you are the sum total of your thoughts to this point in your life, and so am I. That's all we can be. We have spent our lives acting on our ideas or the ideas of others. Ideas are thoughts, and thoughts are everything. How you habitually think is the most important thing about you; it determines everything in your life—your income, your home, your clothes, your education, your speech, your marriage partner, your children—everything except those events that happen to you as a result of what others have thought. When a man is drafted to serve a term in the armed forces, it may not have been his idea at all—far from it. But the fact that he is drafted is the result of an idea reached by those who have the decision-making power.

One idea can make you rich or well-to-do. How many ideas do you think you might get on a Sunday afternoon or morning devoted to thinking? The law of averages begins to swing in your direction when you begin to produce ideas. Let's say you devote an hour a day for six months to producing ideas that tend to explore your personal potential and the wants and needs of those you would be serving. Could you come up with five ideas a day for six months?

My partner, Lloyd Conant, and I, working together, produced a product that has in turn produced sales exceeding twenty-five million dollars. It took us about a month to put it together. A product is an idea.

In Japan there are people who determine the sex of baby chickens with ninety-nine-percent accuracy. They are able to do that even though the sex of baby chicks is ostensibly indistinguishable. But no scientifically ordained system could even approach such astonishing accuracy. The people do it *intuitively.* They simply know which chicks are male and which are female; physical evidence is not required. Individuals training to become chicken-sexers learn the trade only by looking over the shoulders of experienced workers, who themselves cannot explain how they do it.

I mention this to prove the incredible power of intuition. Using our intuition along with our intelligence as a guide can be the best way to produce really super ideas. Make it a habit to carry a folded sheet of paper along with a writing instrument at all times during the day. Ideas tend to make their appearance at unexpected times: in the shower, while driving the car, while having a meal (watch for them at breakfast and lunchtime particularly), while taking a walk. Whenever the mind is in neutral, as I call it, ideas have the opportunity to bubble up to the surface and show themselves. We don't always get our best ideas during think time. But by planting the problem we're working on deep in our mind, it seems that the great subterranean part of our mind works on the idea when we're doing other things. When it hits on a possible answer, it waits for a quiet time to slip it to the top for evaluation. Those ideas should be immediately written down for serious consideration.

I believe that our intuition has a way of plumbing our deep memory, of searching what Teilhard de Chardin called the "noosphere," an invisible layer of human intelligence that forms a mantle around the earth. How it works is a mystery; that it does work we have all seen at times during our lives. Planting a problem or question deep in the unconscious by first turning it every which way during an in-depth conscious attempt to solve it usually results in an answer eventually appearing, completely unbidden, in our consciousness. "Of course!" we often cry. "It's so obvious!" But it was not obvious when we rotated it on the rotisserie of our consciousness. It seems to happen with more frequency for those who count on its happening, who expect it and watch for it as a ship's lookout watches for a light in the darkness.

If you have never experimented with this idea, you will find it endlessly fascinating and enormously rewarding. We often *know* something is right or wrong, just as those Japanese chicken-sexers *know* which chicks are male and which are female. Women tend to be better at it than men; they seem to live closer to their intuition. Perhaps it's because they have historically had to, since they lacked the physical strength to challenge men on a more basic level.

I took my grandson to lunch recently; he is ten years old. As we walked to the car afterward, we passed some young men working with picks and shovels in what appeared to be the demolition of a service station. They were surrounded by dense clouds of dust as, stripped to the waist, they wielded their jackhammers and heavy picks and shoveled the broken concrete. I stopped and, pointing to the young workmen, asked Danny if that's the kind of work he wanted to do when he grew up. He watched them for a moment and shook his head. In the car I explained to Danny that when men and women perform purely physical work, they are not utilizing their greatest resource. Thinking men and women do. We can think better and more profitably, and we can serve more people through ideas than we ever can physically. And it's better for our health, too. Then we have the joy of using our physical bodies for more agreeable pursuits: tennis, golf, sailing, fishing, swimming, camping, hiking, mountain climbing, running, exercising.

"I want to be an archaeologist or an astronomer," Danny said. Whether he finally follows one of those professions or not, Danny is taking the idea of college for granted. The more we know, the better we can think. College isn't always necessary, but it can certainly help the serious student.

William Lyon Phelps, former president of Yale University, used to say, "The most interesting people are the people with the most interesting pictures in their minds." The ideas we hold that direct the course of our lives are the "pictures" in our minds—our art gallery, we might say. And our facial appearance after forty, interestingly enough, is usually a reflection of that art gallery. We are told that our faces after forty are our own responsibilities. It's only natural that they should mirror the contents of our minds. That's what makes so many middle-aged and older people beautiful and handsome, and so many not—and we see a great many of the latter, unfortunately. In the latter case, in all the years of their lives they have failed to put together a gallery of ideas that reflect good cheer, happiness, and hopeful expectation.

Once again, it's the minority that realizes the importance of great ideas in our lives. Ideas are simply everything. A person can have beautiful features, but if great ideas aren't there, the resulting vacuum is quite apparent.

> *I slept and dreamt*
> *That life was joy.*
> *I woke and saw*
> *That life was Duty.*
> *I acted, and behold!*
> *Duty was Joy.*

There's an idea I hold from which I derive a great deal of inner peace and contentment. No doubt when the poet Rabindranath

Tagore of Calcutta, India, worked that poem out, it was the exposure of an idea that meant a great deal to him. Joy—one of the greatest of life's treasures—comes from fulfilling our duty to those we have chosen to serve.

In our free society we choose our work. It isn't forced upon us once we are independent adults. Doing it to the very best of our ability should bring us joy. If it does not, there's something wrong somewhere. Perhaps we're in the wrong work. Or perhaps we have failed to see our work in the proper light. Are we as prepared as we should be? If we don't see opportunity in our work, perhaps it's our vision. We are not looking deeply enough or creatively enough, and so we fail to see all the opportunities for expression available in our present work.

Do we belong to that large group of people that seems to believe it already knows enough? Or that education comes to us while we sleep, or that the education we have is sufficient to stretch over a lifetime? Is it possible that we're expecting maximum service from a minimum inventory?

For many, a diploma or college degree is like a vaccination; in fact it's called "the vaccination theory" of education: once the diploma or degree is in hand, education is over. One college president reported that as he walked toward the podium on commencement day, he overheard a senior saying to another, "Thank God it's over. I'll never open another book as long as I live!" He said those were the saddest words he had ever heard.

Somehow the idea of education had not been sold to that young man; nor did he know the meaning, strangely enough, of the word *commencement.* Education is a lifelong process and should end only when we do, and *commencement* means beginning, not end. Beginning of independence, yes, and also the beginning of the enriching education that will hang the pictures in our minds that determine what we become as persons.

Ideas—the great ideas that move us to be better and greater than we now are—are the deeply imbedded anchors that will hold us in place steadfastly when the great storms of life crash around us. They are the anchors that prevent our being intimidated or diverted from our path by expediency, fad, or demagoguery. Great ideas provide us with a set of sensors that can pick up the dishonest and the phony, revealing the cheap and shoddy and the so-called quick buck. Great ideas provide a lifelong security system for us without disturbing our sense of humor. In fact, our sense of humor is greatly enriched by such ideas, and smiling and laughter become important parts of our days. We are by no means immune to mistakes, but we understand that they are a natural part of growth and reaching into the unknown.

The ideas we hold should be in concert with our goals if our goals are to be successfully achieved.

What is an idea? We say, "I have an idea!" What is that? It is surely more than a neurochemical-electrical response, although it is that, too. An idea is the bringing together of known increments to provide a new result. "Let's go to the beach!" Without a moment's hesitation we take the "known" beach factor, add it to existing transportation facilities, the proper clothing, and possibly a picnic lunch and suggest the resulting "idea" to those we are with at the time. It all happens instantaneously, although all sorts of interconnections are going on in our brains.

The greater our general information, the more combinations we can put together and the greater the reach of our "possibility thinking," as Dr. Robert Schuller calls it. That's why young people should think twice before complaining about school courses "they'll never use as adults." All information of a positive kind has value when we are formulating ideas.

When we set an important goal for ourselves, we present to our minds a problem to be solved, a challenge to be successfully fulfilled. Instantly, far down in the labyrinthine interstices of its vast potential, the mind goes to work to find the information we need to turn that "idea" into reality. We commonly use this astonishing ability for ordinary things. For example, the "idea" of obtaining a particular automobile soon becomes a true automobile that we can drive and wash on warm Sunday afternoons. Perhaps our path from the inception of the idea to the time we get into the automobile, turn the key, and drive away is rather tortuous, even circular, leading first here and then there. More often than not, we get in our own way by doubting the suggestions that filter into our consciousness, only to discover later that they would have been marvelous shortcuts and simplifications of the process if we had only heeded them. But eventually, the idea, the invisible idea becomes sheet steel and glass and upholstery and rubber and, from time to time, a pain in the neck as well. The idea becomes real in our life, even if it takes three years to pay for it.

Everything we obtain during our lifetimes comes to us as a result of that goal-achievement system. Often it consists of nothing more than a trip to the grocery store or a telephone call or a command to a teenager. Idea followed by fulfillment. And as our ideas progress upward in degree, cost, and complication, it is still the same process that will result in fulfillment—or be frightened off by timidity, rationalization or, on occasion, just plain good common sense. Sometimes as we toy or tinker with a delicious idea, our thinking process is flooded by other ideas indicating that that particular delicious idea will have to be postponed for a year or two or maybe five years or even more. Our thinking process tells us— yes, it tells us—that we've made the kind of quantum leap that is out of place if we're to stick to our present plans and ideas. Delaying gratification is often a sign of maturity. That is why a written list is a good idea. Not that we cannot modify that list from time to time. In fact, as we learn how readily such a system brings us fulfillment of our goals, it is not at all unusual to upgrade our list to include levels we may not at first have thought were in the ballpark for us.

Millions of people use this process without giving it a second thought, without understanding the process at all. A system, once understood and tested, can be applied to whatever we seriously consider as goal material. All we need do is leave it to the system. We don't have to fully understand the system in order to use it. The more we try to rationalize and understand every aspect of the working process, the more we tend to get in our own way and limit our potential. It works. Leave it at that.

We become what we think about, but the thinking is up to us. The degree to which people regularly underestimate their capacity for accomplishment is immeasurable. Curiously, we think nothing of the accomplishments of others; that is, what others do we tend to take in stride. But when it comes to setting goals for ourselves, we tend to play things outrageously safe and thus remain within limits embarrassingly narrow. This is especially true if there is some sort of "maintenance" program in effect. That is, if we have a job, even one whose real demands upon us are minimal, we will usually shut down any other efforts to prepare ourselves for

1. Much better, more interesting kind of work.
2. Any sudden emergency that might develop.

I remember watching a television news program in which laid-off workers of a closed Navy yard were being interviewed. The announcer asked, "What are you men going to do now that the Navy yard has closed down?"

The man nearest to him said, "Well, I guess we'll just have to wait for it to reopen again."

Another man said, "I've worked in this Navy yard for twenty-five years. I don't know anything else."

Here were human cattle that could graze in only one pasture, if we are to believe them, and once the pasture was no longer there, they would simply sit down and waste away.

In twenty-five years a person could learn to do heart transplants in his spare time. What were all these people doing with the sixteen hours a day they were not working? What about weekends and vacations? Take a pen and paper and work out the number of hours the average working person is actually on the job during a typical year. Then subtract it from the rest of his or her waking time. If an hour a day were devoted to learning, to doing anything of a valuable nature, the loss of a job would be an incidental thing, perhaps an actual benefit. And how about "think" time?

Anyone who is responsible for providing for a family should have emergency plans A, B, and C—or at least A. Just as a platoon leader in combat must ask himself, "What if the enemy attacks at night? From the rear? On Sunday morning during breakfast?" the family provider should ask, and work out on that legal pad, "What do we do if the company I work for goes out of business or lets me go for any reason?" It's the kind of thinking that a husband and wife can do together as well as separately and as a result have several possible courses of action. And in the meantime, how about that educational program in your main field of interest? You certainly don't want to be five years from now the same as you are today. But the Navy yard workers that were interviewed on that television program were as dumb as they had been twenty years before.

The adults I questioned as a boy of twelve were not one iota smarter than they had been as fifteen-year-olds. They had shut down their thinking and learning apparatus. They were living creatures that responded to stimuli of the most basic kind, and that was all. When they were hungry, they looked about for something to eat. Sleep, food, sex. The rest of the time was absorbed by whatever their world happened to present to them. They laughed at the Jack Benny and Fibber McGee and Molly radio programs. They slapped their knees and shook their heads and laughed and then lapsed back into the partial coma that was their usual waking state.

During the industrial shakeout of the early Eighties we heard this comment again and again: "I worked for that company for thirty years, and now I'm out, just like that!" To hear them talking, one might think they'd made personal sacrifices for the welfare of the company they worked for. They say nothing about the fact that the company paid them for their time on the job and gave them the wherewithal to become anything they might have set their hearts upon becoming. It was a fair arrangement; they were not kidnapped and pressed into servitude. They applied for their jobs and were accepted and were paid for the level of work they performed. There was no agreement to provide them with work until they were too old and infirm to continue. Why didn't they take the possibility of a layoff into consideration and prepare for such an emergency? My friends John and Elsie did. When John was laid off, he and Elsie sold their home in Ohio and moved to Florida, where they retired in the sunshine. If he had been laid off years earlier, they had a little real estate business (buying, refurbishing, and selling) on the side that they could have turned to full time. If they had, they would have become rich. The trouble with John and Elsie was that they, like so many of us, underestimated what they could do working for themselves with the time John was devoting to his job at the steel mill. The job and the regular weekly paycheck were something they, and most people, don't voluntarily give up very often.

But for most, the job and the union become father and mother figures on whom they depend for safety as well as survival. The company is so big, with such big smokestacks, and it employs so many people, and it makes so much steel or whatever—well, it seems as if it will be there forever and all they need to do is show up, do whatever is necessary to keep the job, and then go home again. All the rest of the time, all those zillions of hours, year after year, decade after decade, they can just allow to pass with as little boredom as possible.

Why does no one talk to these people about change? How do such people remain isolated from important information? They are apparently hermetically sealed in ignorance, wrapped and tied in myths and shibboleths. I know. I lived among them.

"Keep reading like that, and you'll ruin your eyes," my father used to say. Reading doesn't hurt the eyes, it's good for them, and it's especially good for the gray matter just behind them.

But all this is gradually changing. Each year more people are moving into the group that thinks.

Ideas are the most important things on earth. And each of us has his or her own idea factory. It comes as standard equipment at birth, the big brain of the *homo sapiens,* the single surviving member of the genus homo. A baby is born, and we hold in our hands a miraculous living creature whose potential is unknown. What will enter that astonishing brain? And from those ingredients, what kind of life will this child fashion?

Peter Drucker has characterized public education as an institution designed for the perpetuation of adolescence. In a conversation I had with three high school girls one morning at breakfast, it was immediately clear that Drucker knew what he was talking about. Of course, chatting with three seventeen-year-old girls for thirty minutes does not constitute an in-depth study, but those with whom I come in contact as clerks in stores and on the telephone seem to offer little in the way of encouragement.

The average man who likes to fish is not a particularly good fisherman; it is believed that ten percent of all fishermen catch eighty percent of all fish caught. The average bowler is not a very good bowler; the average golfer is not a very good golfer; the list goes on. As someone once wrote; "Most of us do only as much as we must do in order to get by without too much discredit." "That's good enough" is a commonly heard remark, and it usually means, "It's really not very good at all." It might pass for the life story of all too many people in the most prosperous nation, with the most yawning opportunities, that the world has ever known.

It's too bad that "Thinking" is not a required course in the public schools. Not "Remembering," which is what most school-work is about, but "Thinking I, II, III, IV," and so on right into the higher realms of university education. It is the highest function of which the human being is capable, and it is not taught in our nation's schools. Thinking is taken for granted.

What every working person should receive upon finishing a training program offered by his or her employer is a tape–cassette program and printed material entitled; "Your Life and Your Work."

In it would be found much of the material we're dealing with here, plus such things as recommended savings plans, emergency planning, and simple aptitude tests designed to help the person find the main area of his or her inherent competence. All this should be fascinating to the person. It opens up all sorts of interesting windows of opportunity: options, options, options—the very things we need if we're to make the kinds of plans that will maximize at least to some degree what we are and what we can do.

The program would have a section headed, "You Have Lost Your Job!" And the section would deal with the subject, "What can you do that the community wants or needs?"—the community being the entire United States and the Free World.

A good friend of mine, Derm Barrett of Ontario, Canada, a business consultant, devoted a total of eight hundred hours to learning Spanish so thoroughly that he now holds business seminars in numerous Latin American countries. It opened up a whole new world of interest and opportunity for him. Eight hundred hours. That's about the same time most working people devote to their jobs in just twenty weeks. Learning the Spanish language means learning, or beginning to learn, about an infinitely rich and fascinating culture. And if anyone needs modern business know-how, it's Latin America. When Derm Barrett explained over the telephone how he had taken on the job of learning Spanish, using his own principles of time management and goal setting, and how rewarding the resulting experiences were and are, I could feel his excitement and enthusiasm. His options had doubled. And how foreigners love us when we speak to them in their native tongue!

Losing a job is often the best thing that can happen to us. It forces on us what we lacked when we were comfortably employed: the energy, imagination, or incentive to look farther afield for bigger and better opportunities. After the initial shock and period of depression, we often find ourselves in work that is much more to our liking, with far more opportunities for advancement than were ever afforded by the old job. Surveys of men and women of singular success have shown that their success hinged directly on the jobs they had left behind. Whether they had quit voluntarily or been fired made no difference. All of the top people in our corporation were formerly employed by other companies. That they are delighted with their present work and higher earnings proves my point. They are in work that is far more interesting, and they are earning more in the way of rewards than ever before in their lives.

There is an excellent theory in business that we should concentrate our thinking not only on things that are going badly or in need of change but also on things that are going best and producing the most revenue. That is where our thinking can have the greatest return. In other words, don't wait until a crisis to think about something. Instead, find ways of improving and upgrading it while it's humming along at its best. And the same kind of thinking works best with us. Don't wait until you've lost a job to start thinking about possible alternatives. Think about them when all is going well, and you're neither under pressure nor suffering from a loss of self-esteem.

So get out your faithful yellow legal pad, and at the top of the page write; "I need better, more interesting, more rewarding work." Under that, you might first ask the question, "Is it to be found with my present company? What can I do for my present company that will make a more important contribution than the work I'm presently doing?"

Another question might be, "If I had my 'druthers,' what would I rather do for a living than anything else in the world?" And here we can make a list of answers that we will later number in the proper order of importance. After each idea we might ask, "Am I now prepared to handle such work?" And, "What will it take to prepare me for such work?"

Another question might be, "What do I know how to do that will best serve the people of this community, or this state, or this country, or the whole world?" Follow this with another list of answers. As we doodle with such ideas, more ideas will come to us. Each new idea spawns new ideas as a fish spawns eggs. And each of the eggs spawns further ideas.

Now we're thinking! Now we're using the equipment we were born to use, and we're putting to work our most valuable possession. Never think in this way without a pen and paper—preferably that yellow pad. Write page after page if you can, as long as the ideas pour out. For some, the ideas will come very slowly and painfully as the process of thinking is explored. But as you force yourself to continue—and thinking, remember, is hard work—you'll find the ideas coming easier and getting better. Don't stop when you get your first exciting idea. Write it down, underscore it, draw a star beside it or a circle around it, then press on for new and better ideas, and you'll find them coming. Work on this in your spare time—early in the morning is best for me—for days and weeks until you have worked out, at the very least, Plan A. Then try for Plan B. Talk the ideas over with your wife or husband and get his or her thinking as well. Soon you'll find yourselves laughing, as delighted as children with your newfound, exciting options.

If you are unaccustomed to writing—and, I'm sorry to say, millions of Americans are—please begin forming the habit with your legal pad. Do not for a moment believe you can remember all the ideas that come swimming to the surface of your consciousness—you must write them down on paper.

If you would like to improve your writing skills, there's a wonderful way to do it: Simply copy from a good book. Write page after page of copy, word after word, making sure you copy all punctuation marks and observe the beginning of new paragraphs. Read aloud as you do so, and you will find your speech improving as your writing becomes easier and more natural. Keep a dictionary by your elbow and look up every word you don't understand. Thirty minutes a day spent in this activity will soon have you writing easily, effortlessly, and enjoyably. You'll find yourself developing a good, legible writing style. Make certain that every word you write is clearly legible. The great W. Somerset Maugham used this system to develop his style as a writer.

I once suggested to the mother of a ten-year-old boy—it was during summer vacation—that she supervise his reading and writing for an hour a day during the summer. I commented that he would go back to school in the fall with a big head start over the rest of his class. She gave me a look she might have used if I had suggested her son learn to speak Chinese. It was apparent that my suggestion would go unheeded, and her son's reading and writing skills would go undeveloped.

Ideas can provide us with autonomy. Ideas can give us freedom. You'll find you have other options, other places you can go.

Good ideas are wondrous, delightful, magical things. They explain why people sometimes earn vastly greater incomes after retirement than they ever did on the jobs to which they so assiduously clung for thirty-five or forty years. With a pension providing a save base below which they know their income cannot fall, they find they have the confidence to pursue the ends and ideas they lacked the courage to pursue when they were working. That's fine. There's nothing carved in marble about when we should do what we ought to do. Any time will do. But we hear such people say, "I should have done this thirty years ago. My God! Think where I would have been today! And think of the fun we would have had!"

The fact is, there is no such thing as security as long as we're alive. Security may only be found at both ends of life—before and after—not during. If we're looking for security during our lifetime, we're looking for something that simply cannot be guaranteed. Insecurity is our natural state; it is not the chimera, the fire-breathing, multilegged, clawed monstrosity we think it is. Insecurity can mean autonomy. It gives us the options we need for interest and challenge in our lives. Insecurity brings out the best in us; it makes us press upon ourselves.

It doesn't hurt to have six months' or a year's income tucked away someplace. That also gives us freedom and autonomy. It gives us time to make a change.

A good idea is an idea that results in a change that is beneficial. And good ideas come in all shapes and sizes.

A good idea means change. And a great money-making good idea needn't come up with anything radically new. There is a larger success lurking in everything that is successful already, through good ideas. If there's a modest business in town that's earning a profit for its owner, it can be improved to earn a much larger profit.

Don't ever say, "I'd like to get to the point where I can start taking things easy." Certainly you can arrange for hard work to be done by others, but keep thinking and planning for the future. If you don't, you'll die. Once people run out of anything interesting to do, they start the long downward slide. They begin to fall apart; things start going wrong. After you die you can take it easy.

The people who live longest are those people who never run out of something to do. They're farmers who have new crops to plant and harvest, fresh cows to milk, and a hundred other chores that demand attention. They're teachers who have a new class every year, or writers who get through writing on one subject and are off on another. And they're people who never run out of ideas. When they finally do come to the end of their lives, they vanish like the image from a suddenly broken motion–picture film.

We learn from reading Ortega that we are the only creatures on the planet who are born to a natural state of disorientation with our world. All other newborn creatures are at home in their new world. Controlled entirely by instincts and reacting automatically to whatever stimuli affect them, they never have to ask, "What will I do?" Why was this preplanned state denied us? We are the only creatures with the power to create our own worlds within the world in which we find ourselves. It's an awesome power indeed. That's why ideas are the greatest things on earth, for it is ideas that shape our lives. Unfortunately, for all too many of us, the lack of great ideas shapes our lives by their absence.

A poet once wrote; "Blessed is the man who has found his

work." A great idea indeed. For the man or woman who has found an unending area of interest to explore, the future is a happy prospect.

And let me repeat another great idea: Such work exists for each of us. If we have not yet found it, we can do no better than to continue our explorations until we do find it.

Still another great idea: Our rewards all the years of our lives will be in direct proportion to our service. We live in order to serve one another.

CHAPTER V

How May I Serve Thee?

When Albert Einstein was asked, "Why are we here?" he replied, "We are here to serve one another only."

Human beings have wants and needs. It is by meeting one or more of the wants and/or needs of others that we serve them. And our rewards—all the years of our lives—will be in relative proportion to our service.

Because of that great idea articulated by Einstein, we can get rid of the "What's in it for me?" approach. That is the hallmark of the immature, the typical small-time operator.

There is a restaurant operated by a family in a lovely coastal town in California. Month after month it hangs on by its fingernails, barely achieving survival. This is in spite of the fact that the food is quite good and the bakery products are excellent. The owners have the idea firmly fixed in their combined mentality that the way to produce the largest profit is to give the least for the best possible price. The idea makes sense on paper. The less one pays for the product one serves and the greater the price charged, the larger will be the profit spread. But this figuring is without the consent of the customer. The customer has an entirely different idea. The customer wants the most for the least amount of money. And the customer makes the decision as to where he or she will spend money.

People vote with their money. They will vote for one place rather than another because they believe they receive a better value. And at the restaurant under discussion, the customer quickly sees that he or she is being charged a maximum price for the least possible product. For example, while most restaurants serve butter on the table, this place butters the bread in the kitchen but does so so sparingly that it's immediately apparent—and it may not be butter at all. It's the same with the other dishes served. The least possible service for the largest possible price. That is to say, the largest price most customers will pay without argument.

So people don't go back to this restaurant a second time. The most profitable customers for any eating establishment are those who come back again and again and bring their friends. This place misses that richest source of trade because of its ridiculous penny-pinching. Month after month, the owners fail to see the cause of their failure.

Another place opened up not long ago in the same general neighborhood, and it's crowded every day. It has a marvelously diversified menu and serves large, delicious servings for the prices charged. The customers at this new place feel they are well served for the money they're spending. My wife and I were having lunch there one day when we noticed a man in street clothes cleaning the table next to ours. We had noticed how busy he was, jumping in wherever he was needed to give the busy waitresses a hand. We introduced ourselves. He was the owner; it was his ninth restaurant in an escalating plan, and he was delighted with it, as we were. It was the culmination of several years of working and planning, and it's a place to be proud of—a real winner. We told him we liked the place, had thoroughly enjoyed our luncheon, and would be back—regularly. As would, I'm sure, the other local people who filled the place.

Kill 'em with service! I forget who said that, but it's the key to success in business. Give your very best, and work at making it better, and give them more than they expect for what they're paying. Do what you do so well that you'll guarantee always getting a disproportionate share of the available business.

Service. We're here to serve each other. And every one of us does who receives anything back in the way of return. Those who do not serve do not receive anything.

I remember as a kid in the Great Depression hearing my elders say, "Someday our ship will come in." Great idea, but only if you've sent one out!

We see the millions who are starving in Africa, and we send money to help them. The drought, the drying up of their lands, the sterile, inefficient governments, the lack of education—all contribute to the inability of these people to serve, so they receive nothing in return except from those of us who can help them in their desperate time of need. They sow not, and they reap not. And they and their children starve and lie helpless in the hot sun and the ubiquitous, swarming flies.

The greatest thing in the world is the opportunity to be of service to others. That's why those of us who live in the more enlightened democracies are so fortunate. There is a whole world out there crying for help, for ideas, for endless products and services. The Third World, yes, of course, but the First and Second worlds as well. The extent of your opportunity to be of service can be said to be the extent of your imagination coupled with your education. And the best place to begin is where you are.

You may already be wonderfully successful at providing a useful service that makes demands on your brains and abilities. But of one fact we can be sure: It can be improved. Another is that there are ways to expand your service to others that you have not thought of. Perhaps your work is so highly personalized that it cannot be increased. That might be true if you're a successful surgeon, sculptor, or painter.

Within the ranks of every profession there can be found a sprinkling of great ones whose expertise and service are of such a quality and range that they do extremely well with the clientele they develop over a period of time. Then there are the very good, the good, the average, and the below average. But it still works out that our rewards, in whatever form we may realize them, are in relation to our service.

We might ask, "Where does the wife of the wage earner fit into this scheme of things? And how about the wife of the dentist or the surgeon or of the man who makes the great knives?" Well, I cannot speak accurately for the wives of others, but let me tell you the part my wife plays in this service-reward affair. My wife and I—Diana and I—provide the setting for each other. Because of Diana and the home she provides for me and all the thousands of things that entails, I can do my best work. More than that, she is my recording engineer and editor. She brings out the best in me. And I bring out the best in her. I know that because she's told me; she knows that she brings out the best in me because I tell her that she does. Without the right woman, nearly every man is a kind of half-man—a truncated sort of being—and his work will seldom repre-sent the best that's in him. And it's the same for a woman. Operating a large, modern household is a full-time job. And when both husband and wife work, which is not the case with Diana, it's even more difficult. My hat is off to those who do.

Men and women are complementary human creatures, and when you find a great match, you have one of the true joys of life: an ongoing job that gives richness and meaning to both of their lives. They serve each other in multitudinous ways. And while each is an original human being, together they form a single unit that reaps the rewards of both of their efforts. They should not be concerned about who earns what. Whatever the husband or wife can produce in whatever way is for the benefit of both as a unit.

The productive ability of a man or woman depends to a surprising extent on the mate and the state of the relationship. Which of them earns the most money should not be a considera-tion, since each is a contributing partner.

So don't ask, "What is a wife worth to a marriage?" You might just as well ask, "What is a husband worth?" It is what they are worth together that makes the difference. And when a person, man or woman, finds the right partner, they're limited only by their dreams.

Together they should ask, "What do we want?" For then they will have an idea of what their service must amount to.

I had been talking about entrepreneurs on my radio broad-casts, when I received a letter saying:

Hold the phone, Nightingale. For every entrepreneur doing his or her own thing in the world there must be several hundred rank–and–file employees quite happy to have a good job. How about the hundreds of thousands of people who work for the Post Office or General Motors or AT&T or Goodyear Tire and Rubber, or the other big multinationals that employ hundreds of thousands of people? Most of them are sober, conscientious, hard-working people who get up every morning and go to work and take care of a job to which they've been assigned. Even more are employed in smaller companies. They don't ask, "Is this the right work for me, or is this the work that best fits my genetic strength." How about them?

All right, fine, how about them? I think they're fine, hardworking people, and we'd be in a hell of a fix without them. But they wouldn't have jobs if it were not for entrepreneurs. Somebody or some group of people had to start the commercial enterprises for which most of these millions of people work. And in most cases they were started by one person with a good idea who was willing to take some risks to prove the idea sound.

And we're all delighted that there are millions of hardworking people who are delighted to have a good job. That's wonderful, and the job and what it produces in the way of income apparently meet their requirements.

But we all serve in some way, or we don't reap a harvest. We must sow in order to reap. The extent of our sowing will determine the size of our harvest, and the quality of our seed will determine the quality of our harvest. Action, reaction—it is the law of the world and the universe, and it reigns in our personal lives just as it does anywhere else.

It is the misunderstanding of this simple fact that keeps millions in a quandary. We hear people say, "So-and-so worked hard every day of his life for forty years and has nothing to show for it." In that case, he made some serious mistakes. He should be quite well-to-do by now. He was either in the wrong work or failed to see the opportunities that lurked within it.

Our postman serves us loyally and well. I don't know if our postman has ever asked himself, "Is this the right work for me?" or, "Is this the work that best fits my genetic strength?" But he seems quite happy with his job with the Post Office. And perhaps he has a consuming hobby that fills his spare time. Perhaps that's all he and his wife need.

I called our local postmaster to find out how many homes or places of business the average postperson serves and was told it would average out between 400 and 650. Let's say 500. That's service of a high order, indeed, when stretched over a working career.

Everyone who needs to earn a living should ask himself or herself; "How can I best serve other people?" If we're not an Albert Einstein or a Barbra Streisand or a Joe Montana or a Carroll O'Connor—that is, if we don't already know, deep down in the very fiber of our being, what we're supposed to do—we need to take Socrates's advice and begin an in-depth examination of ourselves. We might begin by thinking about our childhood: What were we attracted to? When we played with other children, did we want to be the captain all the time, the king of the mountain, or were we delighted to be one of the crew? In our daydreams, what recurring fantasy appeared? What were we especially good at in school? Which class did we most enjoy?

Another excellent research source is the autograph book we passed around the class at graduations from elementary and junior high school. Our friends and classmates often saw our strong point even if we took it for granted or weren't aware of it.

I was astonished many years ago to uncover my old autograph book and find nearly every entry saying something like, "Good luck, Earl Nightingale, the storyteller." I was astonished because I had no recollection whatever of having told stories to the other kids. After thinking about it, I realized that, being something of an omnivorous reader, I must have shared some of the stories I read with my classmates. But to this day I have no recollection of doing anything of the kind. Yet there are all those entries: "Good luck, Earl Nightingale, the storyteller."

My classmates in junior high school were actually writing down in my autograph book the career that I should follow. Perhaps they were good enough to do the same for you.

Human genetics is a fascinating subject. Each of us can do so many things, it's difficult for many people to identify a single strong point, a specialty. Yet there is something each of us can do better than other things, that we enjoy more than other things, that we would rather spend the rest of our lives doing than other things.

If our strong point is management, perhaps it isn't important what the people we manage produce. A manager is one who makes things happen. An administrator is one who oversees or manages an already successful organization. If the organization begins to head downhill, the administrator will often ride all the way down to the final collapse, administering as he does so. Not the manager. The minute he sees trouble, he begins doing something about it. And the good manager does something about the organization on a regular basis, even when it's prospering. The manager is happy in the presence of challenge and change. The administrator is not.

How do you feel about change? Do you see change leading to bigger and better things, to the solutions of presently pressing problems? Or do you tend to view change as a threat to the status quo?

The entrepreneur is one who can live in a state of risk and challenge. In fact the entrepreneur is at his or her best in such a state. All unusual success is in some degree related to risk.

When John and Elsie discovered they could earn sizable profits by buying up old homes in good neighborhoods and refurbishing them to then sell at a profit, they would have been wise to quit the job at the steel mill and go into the real estate business full time. But their natures wouldn't allow it. Something might go wrong. The real estate market might go completely to pot in a real recession and they'd be without income and without a job. That weekly paycheck from the good old steel company was their security—they thought. But the American steel industry generally did not keep up with the changing shape of the world economy (change of any sort was fought hammer and tong by the steel unions as well as by entrenched management), and Japan's new steel mills, built after World War II, began producing quality steel at much lower prices. Even John, in management, with his three decades of loyal attendance, was dropped from the payroll. But by that time he had his pension, and he and Elsie had their very substantial savings and investment account. They were then as free as the happy birds they now are in their condominium in Florida. John and Elsie were part-time entrepreneurs, and it paid off for them.

There are also entrepreneurs within large organizations, often called *intrapreneurs*. In fact there are much more of them now than ever before in business history. More and more companies are helping employees with good ideas set up operations within the company. In that way the company provides everything the new idea needs in the way of start-up funds, operating capital, plant, and equipment, as well as all the help they need. Soon such people find themselves heads of growing, profitable divisions under their company's umbrella and name, and they are rewarded accordingly.

John and Elsie could not have operated their real estate refurbishing operation within the steel company he worked for. It was completely out of the company's line. But intrepreneuring is something for everyone who works for wages to think about.

When we think about how we might better serve others, we do not necessarily have to think in terms of large numbers of customers. After all, how many customers did John and Elsie need for their real estate operation? A dozen? And how about W. D. "Bo" Randall and his magnificent knives? He's got a four-year waiting list, and it takes twelve hours to make his lowest-priced knife.

That's what I call the Rolls-Royce category. If you have a product for which you can charge enough, you don't have to produce and sell all that many of them to have a good business. There's a jeweler named Kocek in Carmel, California, who makes beautiful, one-of-a-kind jewelry. He's in a business he loves, has a beautiful downtown store, and has been doing quite nicely for many years.

He's a very successful man, but he doesn't have as many customers as, say, Kellogg's does. What a winner their Corn Flakes have been! And Ritz Crackers for Nabisco! Two now-ancient products that were such good ideas to begin with, they're still at the top of the pile.

There is so much to do and so many millions to serve; all you need is one good idea. How many ideas can you get on a quiet weekend? You only need one good one. How many ideas can you get if you devote an hour a day to creative thinking? As you think about your ideas, remember the idea of service. Your idea must serve the needs or wants of a segment of the total market sufficient to meet your needs. You don't need everybody. Not even Kellogg or Nabisco has everybody.

Relatively few people think deliberately and creatively on a regular basis. We tend to stop thinking the minute we have an idea of sufficient merit to meet our needs. The person with just one good idea is a thousand times better off than the person with no good ideas. But he or she is not nearly as successful or full of fun and interest as the person who keeps getting better ones. What you want is an idea good enough to build on. Old Henry Ford's idea was to build a car the average working man could afford. He did that and became one of the world's richest men. But look at the Ford products that can be obtained today!

IBM started with those old funny punchcards, and so it grew. I can remember when my late partner, Lloyd Conant, and I would spend hours thinking of ways in which we could get our company sales up to a million dollars a year. Now we're creeping up on a million dollars a week, and by the time you read this we may well have surpassed that goal. We serve more people with more products than we even imagined fifteen or twenty years ago.

The cumulative effects of days spent paying attention to a good idea are enormous. Like a great wave, an idea has its beginning far at sea. At first it's barely perceptible. But as it nears the continent and the water grows shallower, the wave grows, and finally, in undulating and translucent power, it rises up and curls into booming foam on the shore. And when that happens to your idea, when you see it fully accepted and wonderfully successful, it is one of the greatest joys of life. It's as moving as watching one of your children graduate from college.

When you're thinking of creative ways to serve, either the Rolls-Royce or the Nabisco system will do. That is, a smaller market for an expensive, high-quality product, or an unlimited market for a low-priced product. The same kind of thinking can apply to services as well as products.

You can play around with both ideas, as well as one involving a medium-priced product or service. That is the fastest-growing market in the United States and the one the Japanese are now addressing in the business of cars. When they were asked to reduce the number of cars sold to the U.S. market, the Japanese complied by shipping fewer but more expensive cars. They increased their dollar volume considerably while substantially reducing the number of cars exported. A much better idea for the American market.

"There's more than one way to skin a cat!" I have no idea where that nauseating cliché came from, but it's a good idea when applied to problems. "They want us to ship fewer cars next year?

Okay, let's ship fewer cars, but let's make them better, fancier, more expensive models. In that way we solve their problem and ours at the same time."

There is usually a serendipitous solution to apparently threatening problems. In fact, in solving tough problems, we usually find we're better off than we would have been if the problem had not appeared.

"There's more than one way to skin a cat." If it won't work one way, it will work another way. Remember the idea of service. As Einstein said, "We are here to serve others only." Throw yourself into that idea. "How can we be of service, or how best can we serve?" And keep serving. And if your company grows and you find yourself with a board of directors, have murals painted on the wall of the boardroom depicting your customers in all walks of life and all ages. The theme of every meeting should be, "Will this result in our providing better service to those we have chosen of our own free will to serve?"

Your customers should come first, your employees second. You should be at the end of the line looking at what's left over. Your customers and employees will take wonderful care of you if you will first take wonderful care of them.

Service is the answer, service to everyone who is important to us. To our loved ones, most certainly to our customers, and then to our employees. They will provide us with everything we could possibly want in return.

That's the way it works.

CHAPTER VI

Great Expectations

To ask, "What is the role of attitude in a person's success or failure?" is much like asking, "What is the role of granite in the Himalayas?" or "What is the role of H_2O in the Pacific Ocean?"

Attitude comes very close to being everything about success or failure. With a great attitude, a person can succeed though he may start with very little else. Attitude makes the sale—or loses it.

What is attitude? The dictionary describes it as a matter of bearing or mood. But it's much more than that. Attitude is what sets the stage for what we want or expect to happen. The person who goes through life, as millions do, saying, "With my luck the whole thing will go down the toilet!" goes down the toilet over and over again. Attitude sets the stage for failure; if someone expects failure and he or she thinks about failing, then he or she fails over and over again. People can have a great education, but if they also have a poor attitude, they will almost certainly fail.

An attitude that demands excellence results in excellence. You and I can see to it that we maintain an attitude of great expectations. It's more fun and so much more interesting to adopt and keep such an attitude, and it always results in our reaching new levels of achievement.

We are not born with a drive for excellence in our lives and work. That quality comes from learning or experience or both. But we are born with exuberance and curiosity, and when these qualities are combined with great expectations, we can expect marvelous results. We try harder, and we put more of ourselves into what we do when we have an attitude of great expectations. "That's good enough" won't do—not for a moment.

An expectant attitude, an attitude that expects good things to happen, that expects success, has an uncanny way of shaping future events and bringing together the most astonishing coincidences. The right people appear at the proper time, and suddenly other people around us are infected by our ideas and spirit; their morale goes up, and they're as infected with the idea of excellence and success as we are. A great attitude is marvelously infectious. It can spread throughout an entire company or organization. If there are great attitudes at the top of an organization, there will be great attitudes throughout the organization. Everyone begins putting more of himself and herself into the effort.

An American woman was once so impressed by the ragout at a fine restaurant in Paris, she asked the chef if he would give her the recipe. He was happy to comply. A couple of years later, back in the same restaurant, the woman chided the chef for not having given her the complete recipe for the ragout. "It doesn't taste as good as yours," she told him.

The chef went over the recipe again with her, and when she told him she had followed it to the letter, he looked at her for a long moment and then said, "Madame, perhaps you left out the most important ingredient of all. Perhaps you forgot to throw yourself into the ragout."

That's the difference that a great attitude can make, regardless of what we happen to be doing. Roger Staubach, one of the greatest quarterbacks in National Football League history, called me one morning and asked if I would write the foreword to the book he was working on. Long a fan of Staubach's and of the Dallas Cowboys, I told him I'd be delighted and asked that he send me a copy of the manuscript. Later, in conversation with him, we talked about the role of the quarterback in leading the team. He mentioned that a winning attitude on the part of the quarterback, in his posture, his facial expression, his voice, the plays he calls, in his entire demeanor, can do more than anything else to lift the spirits of the team for the extra effort required. "So much of sports is a mental game," he went on to say. And here again, "we become what we think about" in our success or failure.

Life is a game, too, and in many ways it is much like the game of American football or golf or tennis. Practically all of life is a mental game. Our attitude directs our minds, and our minds direct us. But it is our attitude, more than any other factor, that will determine our success or failure. An attitude that says, "We can do this," will do more than any other single factor in getting the job done, whatever it is.

Our true attitude toward something has a palpable effect on those about us; it can even affect animals. A horse, for example, is affected by the attitude of its rider and will often react accordingly. It's as though we send out an aura or vibrations that are picked up by those about us. Women tend to be particularly sensitive to the auras or radiations of others. We "feel" good about a person, or we "feel" nervous or ill at ease, even suspicious. Most husbands have at one time or another experienced their wives saying to them after having met someone, "I don't trust that person. There's something fishy about him." And their appraisal is often later confirmed.

Many times over the years I've found myself overtipping a waiter or waitress who has a good attitude about doing the job. A friendly, happy, positive attitude often makes up for so-so food or other mistakes that might have ruined a dinner, had the attitude been average or poor. People who serve the public and depend on tips for part of their income can often double their tip income simply by improving their attitudes. They will also cut down on the number of complaints.

It is a fact of life that the great majority of people begin their days in neutral as far as attitude is concerned, and they depend on whatever stimuli they encounter to set the attitude-tone for them. If things go well and it's a beautiful day, their attitude may be fine; if things go wrong or it's cold and raining, their attitude will reflect that also. Not understanding the importance of a great attitude and what it can mean to us, they put their attitudes in the hands of others or the elements and live accordingly. It is a reactive kind of life, not a very satisfactory sort of existence.

And it's all the worse for those millions living in bleak and dismal surroundings. There is little to generate a happy, expectant attitude. Add to that the depressing aspects of most public transportation, and by the time the workday begins, expectations are lagging at best. This is best seen in the large Eastern cities of the United States. And the course of their day will usually bear out their expectations. Their attitudes broadcast their expectations, as do their facial expressions and postures. And so the flight attendant's asides to her co-worker as the passengers begin filling the jetway, "Here come the animals!"

Yet it is a day of their lives—a day filled with opportunities for success, adventure, and who knows what synchronistic and serendipitous wonders for the person with great expectations. If any one of them knew it was to be his or her last day of life, how sweet, how precious it would suddenly become—how filled with color and interesting faces and sounds! How great it would suddenly become to be of service and experience every minute of the day.

I recall the day when the American hostages, held for so many months in Iran, were returned to the United States. I recall the looks on their faces, the way many of them kissed the tarmac on disembarking from the plane. Blessed freedom, just to be home again. As Mr. Levin, the correspondent who escaped after eleven months of captivity, shouted upon his return, "I'm a born-again American!"

How sweet it is after it's been taken away for a time! Yet how many millions of us take our days for granted and go about them grudgingly, defensively, with an attitude that says, "Do unto others before they can do unto you."

Thousands of people, on discovering what a change in attitude can mean for them, actually do become born-again Americans, or born-again Canadians, or born-again whatever nationality they happen to be. Because there is no fragment of this freedom of ours that cannot be turned into the success we seek. There are no jobs so humble that they do not have hidden within them the opportunity for greatness and all the success we could possibly want. But it takes an expectant attitude to see it. That kind of attitude draws back the curtains of ordinariness that cloak the work of the majority and exposes the possibilities within.

You and I are on a kind of holiday on earth. Out of the mystery we appear, to share our lives with the other living things on this small blue blessed planet. We spend time here before merging back into the mystery once again. During this time, let us enjoy ourselves to the fullest. To do that, we need to examine ourselves, as wise old Socrates admonished us, and discover what we are best equipped to give for the journey's fare. There is really no good excuse for not doing that which we most want to do, nor for not enjoying to the fullest those experiences we find to our liking. They make the holiday all the more interesting and rewarding. Being on this holiday, there are few times that warrant genuine sadness, unless we take upon our shoulders the problems and miseries of the entire world. That is futile. We need only brighten the corner where we are to the very best of our abilities. That is our part of the bargain, to give it our best during the time we dedicate to service. And the rest we can enjoy with those we love and with whom we share our lives.

My wife and I have lived in Carmel, California, for a number of years. Since my work involves reading, research, and writing, it makes little difference where I live. But it is generally acknowledged by those who have experienced the Monterey Peninsula of California that it is one of the most delightful and beautiful places on the planet to live. Millions of people visit Monterey, Carmel, Pebble Beach, and Pacific Grove each year. They enjoy the "Seventeen-Mile Drive" and the charming village of Carmel, set in its own forest on one of the country's most beautiful stretches of coastline. And for many years, the golfers of the nation watched the famous Bing Crosby Golf Tournament telecast from the Pebble Beach Golf Course, surely one of the most interesting, beautiful, and spectacular golf courses in the world.

When the people Diana and I meet on our frequent travels around the world learn that we live in Carmel they invariably comment on how fortunate we are to live in such a beautiful place. How fortunate we are—as if our living in Carmel were some sort of cosmic accident. We live in Carmel because we chose to live there, and we chose to live there precisely because of the great beauty of the place and its delightfully cool summers. "Hey, you lucky guys," they'll say.

Of course we are fortunate and we are lucky—astonishingly so. But it's a part of our plan. It's not a result of capricious chance. We also have a home in southwest Florida, a beautiful and bountiful place where we can have a boat and do some fishing and exploring of the surrounding seas. We're on a holiday, we two. How about you? Do you live where you live because you chose to live there, or because your parents chose to live there? Is it your holiday or theirs?

No matter where one lives in the United States or Canada, he or she is among the most fortunate of human beings because of our liberty, our space, and our bounty. But if we're in charge of this holiday, it should be up to us to decide where we're going to spend it. There's as much opportunity in Norwalk, Connecticut, as there is in Dallas, Texas. Have you ever heard of Stew Leonard, the dairy–store operator? Stew Leonard has the busiest and most profitable store in the world. It's built around his milk–processing plant. People from a hundred miles around do their shopping at Stew Leonard's. He has buses bring older people, free, to his store from the surrounding areas so that they can do their shopping and enjoy his marvelous products and prices. Everything that is sold in Stew Leonard's store is sold in greater volume than in any other store in the world. He sells more chocolate–chip cookies and ice-cream cones than anyone else in the world, and it's the same for milk, cottage cheese and cream, meat products, and the hundreds of other things he sells. He sells salads by the ton each week! And Stew Leonard, a former milk-delivery-route man, lives in Norwalk, Connecticut.

Where do you live? What are you doing there? And what is your attitude toward this holiday we call life on earth? Stew Leonard's attitude is marvelous. I know because I called him on the telephone the other morning, and we had a long talk. He's a happy guy because he's made the most of himself.

What a world of meaning is in that sentence, "He's made the most of himself." I should have added, "So far." He told me he's building another store in another community. I hope he builds them all over the country if he can maintain the kind of quality enjoyed by his customers at the Norwalk store.

Just as there is no job that does not have the seeds of greatness lurking somewhere within it (remember, Stew Leonard was a milkman), there is no community that does not offer the same opportunity. I'm sure most of the people in the world have never heard of Norwalk, Connecticut. Most of the people in the United States have never heard of it. But many wonderful things have been done there by people who chose to do a bit more with their holidays on earth.

There is much too much to see and do. As Robert Frost says, "I have promises to keep/And miles to go before I sleep." Another of his poems is entitled, "Happiness Makes Up in Height What It Lacks in Length."

Thinking of our lives as holidays on earth can change our mood or attitude from one of defensiveness—survival at all costs— to one of happy exploration: the exploration of ourselves and the world in which we find ourselves. Each of us determines his or her own value by what we choose to do, how we choose to serve.

I spent twenty-three years of my life residing in Chicago and its environs. Talk about Opportunity City! Chicago always has been and remains to this day one of the great boomtowns and opportunity centers in the world. Nor can a more interesting population mix be found anywhere. It's the world in a microcosm, and it teems with customers for everything under the sun.

Wherever there are other human beings, there's opportunity. And with modern communication, you could do well living wherever you might choose to live. But choose! You can reach as many millions as you choose to reach through advertising or direct mail, even if you live in Weed, California, or Cleveland, Florida; in Oil Trough, Arkansas, or Nowhere, Arizona. How about a villa on one of the Greek islands or the Italian Riviera? Portofino is a beautiful place; have you considered living abroad for a few years? The greatest opportunity in the world is wherever you happen to be. Sit down with your yellow legal pad and make some notes. Assess your attitude. Ask your friends what they think of your general attitude; ask your children or your wife or your husband.

The earth was here for billions of years before you were born, and it will be here for billions of years after you have died. You're on vacation—you're on a holiday here. Life itself is yours for a while.

You will be happy to the extent of your service to others, to the proportion of yourself you give away.

Now, about that attitude of yours.

To ask, "What is the role of attitude in a person's success or failure?" is much like asking, "What is the role of granite in the Himalayas, or the role of H_2O in the Pacific Ocean?" It is almost everything. You are the rest.

CHAPTER VII

Stay with It

I always felt I was pretty good in the perseverance department. After all, writing a radio program every day for twenty-six years—that's about nine thousand radio programs, researched or thought of and then written one word at a time on a typewriter before being recorded for broadcast—6,300,000 words, one word at a time. It doesn't exactly label me a fly-by-night kind of person. But next to Diana, when it comes to perseverance, I'm still in kindergarten. She is simply implacable. So between us, setting and reaching goals, no matter what their degree of difficulty, is not a matter for questioning. We do it.

We've all seen motion pictures in which the hero, mustering that last cubic centimeter of strength, crawls over the final sand dune to see, to his delighted astonishment, a shady oasis with abundant fresh water and the cheerful leader of a camel train who volunteers to give him a free ride back to civilization and ultimate victory. It is mustering that last bit of energy, for just one more try and then, after that, just one more, that often leads to victory in real life.

"Nothing takes the place of persistence." Do you remember that little essay so popular thirty or forty years ago? It's true—nothing takes the place of persistence, once you know that what you're seeking is right for you.

When I resigned my cushy job at CBS in Chicago in 1950 and started my own program on WGN, I also agreed to help sell time on my show by calling on advertising agencies. So I would write my next day's program at night, at home, then first thing the next morning I would start hitting the advertising agencies to tell them why their clients should be advertising on my daily radio program. I was completely unknown in the Chicago market or anywhere else; my time on the air amounted to just fifteen minutes each afternoon. My prospects would say, "No, sorry, your program is not in 'drive time'"—a ridiculous cliché, since at *any* time in Chicago there were a zillion cars on the roads and highways, to say nothing of the ten zillion people listening to their radios at home in about a six-state area. But that's the kind of answer I got, and so I became acquainted with the word *no.* After making calls on numerous agencies and getting nothing but nos, I would then rush to my tiny office in the Tribune Tower, get my program ready for broadcasting, and when the red light came on, I had to be cheerful!

Month after month I made the rounds, and as I did, my thoughts often drifted back to those untroubled days in the quiet, air-conditioned studios at CBS, when all that was expected of me was the occasional exercise of my larynx.

"Stay with it," I would tell myself. One time I surprised a gentleman standing next to me in the men's room of a Chicago high-rise by actually muttering it aloud.

"What was that? Sorry, I didn't here you very well."

"What? Oh! nothing. Nothing at all. Just talking to myself, I suppose."

Embarrassing, yes, but no less important for that. "Stay with it!" I knew that if I could just stay with it long enough to earn the respect and notice of the Chicago advertising community, I could succeed at my project. "Stay with it," I would say to myself on those cold, snowy mornings and hot, humid summer days. "Stay with it," I would say to myself on those heartbreakingly beautiful mornings when all in the world I wanted to do was play hookey, play golf, or walk along the lakefront in the park. So I made my calls and I broadcast my programs and I heard otherwise intelligent agency people say to me, "Radio doesn't work for us."

I would then say, "When you say 'Radio doesn't work for us,' it's the same as a commanding general saying, 'Tanks don't work for us,' or 'Air strikes don't work for us.' The effective commander makes best use of all forces available to him, and so does the good advertising executive. What do you mean, 'Radio doesn't work for us'? What radio? Which radio? Which program or personality? Surely some facet of an industry as broad, pervasive, and successful as American radio will work for you. In fact, my program will work for you in Chicago; I will see to it that my program does a good job for you and returns sales in many times the volume of its small cost."

So I would win the argument and lose the sale. Once he had made his statement, he had to stand behind it or run the risk of being a reasonable, flexible, intelligent advertising executive, and that was, indeed, a great deal to expect.

It was in Kroch's old bookstore on Michigan Avenue that I found the copy of *Think and Grow Rich* by Napoleon Hill in which I found the six-word secret to success I had been searching for for so many years. I took the book back into Kroch's bookstore and pigeon-holed Adolph Kroch himself.

"Buy time on my radio program, and I'll sell this book by the thousands of copies," I said.

"We've tried radio. It doesn't work for us," he replied.

"Don't confuse my radio program with the word *radio*. My program will work for you with this book and with other books in your store as well."

"I'll tell you what I'll do," he said. "I'll give forty cents a copy for every copy of the book you sell."

I was not supposed to work on commission; I was supposed to bring in contracts: thirteen-week, twenty-six-week or fifty-two-week contracts.

"You've got a deal," I said.

Not since the publication of *Gone with the Wind* had old man Kroch seen orders for a book come in the way they came in for the next few weeks. As he wrote out my very sizable checks for thousands of orders at forty cents a copy, he wished he'd followed my advice and simply bought air time on my program; it would have been infinitely cheaper. He promptly rectified the matter. I got him to write a letter saying what my program had accomplished for him, and from that time on, with the kind of proof that the followers of the world need before they will make a move, my program began to attract sponsors. It grew from fifteen minutes a day to a half-hour, then to a full hour, then to an hour in the afternoon and a half-hour in the morning, then to an additional half-hour daily television program—all happily sponsored.

On the program I talked about things I found to be interesting: books, philosophy, people, events. My only rule for subject matter was that it had to be interesting to me. If it was interesting to me, I felt it would be interesting to a large section of the radio audience, and I was right. I have long thought it shameful the way the broadcasting industry has underestimated the listener. I think the radio listener wants more than repeated news, weather, and music. Radio is certainly one of the greatest educational opportunities in the world, the only rule being: "Keep it interesting."

My habit of muttering to myself, "Stay with it!" had paid off, just as it always does. The world is full of those who "tried" to get out of the doldrums and, meeting with difficulty and repeated turn-downs, retreated back to the big crowd. What's really amazing are the number who have made sorties into a business of their own, then failed and fell back, never to try again. Why should succeeding at a business of one's own be easier than learning to ski or play the piano? We are likely to fail at first—it's part of the learning process—but it's no reason to give up. We learn something important from every failure; it's staying with it that separates the winners from the losers.

And "staying with it" applies to so much that is good and healthful in life. Failures aren't the end of the world, far from it. If they were, no human being would ever learn to walk or speak or ride a bicycle or obtain an education. We take early failures for granted in so many things; yet when we attempt something as adults, we become self-conscious. We become concerned about what our friends and acquaintances might think.

Perseverance is another word for faith!

Many years ago I was riding in a taxi in Chicago's Loop area. I remember the spot well: Marshall Field's department store was there on the right. My driver commented that a friend of his, another cab driver, had started to go into a business of his own.

"But I talked him out of it," my driver said. "I told him that ninety-five percent of all new businesses fail and that he'd lose his shirt."

"What did he do?" I asked.

"He's back to drivin' a cab where he belongs." My driver chuckled.

"Where did you get the statistic that ninety-five percent of all new business ventures fail?" I asked.

"What? Why, everybody knows that."

"You were wrong. Ninety-five percent of new businesses do not fail. And let me ask you this: If your friend had gone into a business of his own and failed, could he have got his job back driving a cab?"

"Oh, sure."

"Then he didn't have anything to lose by trying, did he?"

"He might have lost some money."

"But what if he had succeeded? What if he had found his way out of cab driving into a successful and prosperous career as a businessman, like Marshall Field or the founders of all the businesses in Chicago? You didn't do him a favor; you kept him from what might have been a wonderful success."

The silence, even in Chicago's Loop, was suddenly deafening.

"I guess I didn't think of it like that."

"Giving advice to friends doesn't require thinking," I commented. "All you have to do is open your mouth, and all the clichés and myths and half-truths just come pouring out. I heard it all as a kid."

"You have your own business?"

"Yes, I do."

He just shook his head.

Friends often seem to have a vested interest in keeping us in their company. Any talk on our part of doing something that will elevate us to a new plateau can start the myth machine. That is not true with special friends. There are friends who are completely unselfish in their desire to see us do well, who take pride in our accomplishments. But when you get advice, consider the source. What are his or her qualifications for commenting on something you want very much to do? Best of all, don't talk about it! Just do it. And if it fails, do it again and again until you get it right. If you've made up your mind to do something, and if you are fully committed, you're going to do it. A year or so devoted to planning, studying, and marshaling your resources is certainly a good idea.

The story of success in all fields is the story of persistence, perseverance, doggedness, bullheadedness, stubborn tenaciousness. There! That should handle the matter.

But as Eric Hoffer wrote: "There are many who find a good alibi far more attractive than an achievement. For an achievement does not settle anything permanently. We still have to prove that we are as good today as we were yesterday.

"But when we have a valid alibi for not achieving anything, we are fixed, so to speak, for life. Moreover, when we have an alibi for not writing a book and not painting a picture and so on, we have an alibi for not writing the greatest book and not painting the greatest picture. Small wonder that the effort expended and the punishment endured in obtaining a good alibi often exceed the effort and grief requisite for the attainment of a most marked achievement."

How true that is! We've all seen men begging for money with physical handicaps no worse than those suffered by many who are working hard and supporting a family. For one, it's a reason to try all the harder; for the other, it's an alibi for begging.

I'm sure we're all guilty from time to time of using convenient alibis for not doing some of the things we might do. But if we're honest with ourselves, we don't make it a way of life. But there are many who do just that and live lives far below the levels of attainment they might know. They cling to their alibis frantically, with both hands, forcing themselves to close their eyes and ears to the truth that surges about them.

One time the late Dr. Maxwell Maltz, the plastic surgeon who achieved a great deal of fame through his book *Psycho-Cybernetics*, dropped by my office for a chat and lunch. We fell to talking about his favorite subject: namely, how a person can come to grips with himself or herself, develop a healthy self-image, and find freedom in the world.

At that time, Dr. Maltz, whom we called Uncle Max, was seventy-two years old. He was as busy as he had ever been in his life, traveling from one end of the world to the other, making speeches, returning to his New York offices for surgery commitments, and starting all sorts of new projects along the way.

He told me he had discovered four important steps that a

person can take on a regular basis to form new habits that can build a healthy new self-image. As he talked at lunch, I made notes. Here are his four points in the order in which he gave them to me:

1. Forgive others, with no strings attached. Clean the slate absolutely by forgiving every person against whom you might hold some kind of grudge. Do this for your own sake, your own peace of mind. We don't hurt others when we hold hatred toward them; we hurt ourselves. And we can hurt ourselves seriously by allowing hatred to fester in our consciousness. So forgive others—all others. If you cannot take this first step, you can forget the rest—you haven't grown up yet.

2. Forgive yourself. See yourself with kind eyes. Try to forget completely all the idiotic things you've done, the pain you've given to others, the embarrassments you've suffered, the mistakes you've made in the past. Again, wipe the slate clean. Look in the mirror and forgive yourself. Practice this, and you can actually pull it off. It's not easy to forgive ourselves. We are our own worst critics, and we can be much tougher on ourselves than we are on others. But the fact is, blame doesn't help—it's a destructive emotion.

3. See yourself at your best. As Dr. Maltz put it, "We can start the day in frustration or confidence, take your pick. The intelligent thing to do is pick confidence, if it's at all possible." There are bad days, but it's better to begin the day in a confident mood than in a mood of frustration.

4. Keep up with yourself; don't worry about what others are doing or what others have. Keep your pace—it's different from the pace of others. It's faster than some, slower than others. Forget the Joneses, and don't feel guilty about moving ahead of some of your contemporaries. The person who deliberately holds himself down to a slower pace just to be one of the gang is a fool. Keep up with yourself. Live the life you want to live; earn what you want to earn; do what you want to do. Live your own life, and don't be too concerned about how others are living theirs.

Max told me that day at lunch that he called these the four steps to a healthy self-image:

1. Forgive others.
2. Forgive yourself.
3. See yourself at your best—choose confidence instead of frustration.
4. Keep up with yourself, march to your own drummer, go at your own pace and don't worry about what others are doing.

Very good advice from a distinguished physician.

You may wonder why a cosmetic surgeon, a man who put people back together after accidents and gun battles, was so interested in the idea of self-esteem. It was because he found in his practice that although he could remove disfiguring scars, birth-marks, and other anomalies from the faces and bodies of his patients, they often kept the same crippled opinions of themselves even after the surgery had healed. And when that happened, the surgery had failed. He found that unless he could change the inner person to match the new outer person, the individual remained crippled. It's another area where perseverance is required. And as we grow into new persons, achieving ever-higher goals, we need to become on the inside the person we are becoming on the outside.

Staying with our plans despite repeated setbacks tends to build inner character, just as it draws maturity on our faces.

I came across a story about a boy named Sparky. School was all but impossible for Sparky. He failed every subject in the eighth grade. He flunked physics in high school. Receiving a flat zero in the course, he distinguished himself as the worst physics student in the school's history. He also flunked Latin and algebra and English. He didn't do much better in sports. Although he did manage to make the school golf team, he promptly lost the only important match of the year. There was a consolation match. He lost that, too.

Throughout his youth Sparky was awkward socially. He was not actually disliked by the other students; no one cared that much. He was astonished if a classmate ever said hello to him outside school hours. No way to tell how he might have done at dating. In high school, Sparky never once asked a girl out. He was too afraid of being turned down.

Sparky was a loser. He, his classmates—everyone knew it. So he rolled with it. Sparky made up his mind early in life that if things were meant to work out, they would. Otherwise he would content himself with what appeared to be his inevitable mediocrity.

But one thing was important to Sparky: drawing. He was proud of his own artwork. Of course, no one else appreciated it. In his senior year of high school, he submitted some cartoons to the editors of his class yearbook. They were turned down. Despite this particularly painful rejection, Sparky was so convinced of his ability that he decided to become a professional artist.

Upon graduating from high school, he wrote a letter to Walt Disney Studios. He was told to send some samples of his artwork, and the subject matter for a cartoon was suggested. Sparky drew the proposed cartoon. He spent a great deal of time on it and on the other drawings. Finally the reply from Disney Studios came—he had been rejected once again. Another loss for the loser.

So Sparky wrote his own autobiography in cartoons. He described his childhood self, a little-boy loser and chronic under-achiever. The cartoon character would soon become famous all over the world. For Sparky, the boy who failed every subject in the eighth grade and whose work was rejected again and again, was Charles Schulz. He created the "Peanuts" comic strip and the little cartoon boy whose kite would never fly and who never succeeded in kicking the football—Charlie Brown.

Perseverance—nothing can take its place. There is a place for every person who will persevere; there is a large success lurking in everything we do. And it's not just our success we're talking about here. Millions of people have been cheered by and seen themselves in Charlie Brown. There's a Lucy who will snatch that football away in every neighborhood. She's a good girl, really; she just loves to frustrate Charlie Brown. Charles Schulz succeeded beyond his most sanguine imagination, and he earned and deserved that success. Perhaps he failed at everything else he tried because his talent and humor were so complete, so wonderfully successful, when he finally found what it was he was supposed to do.

We tend to be an instant-gratification society. Pick the home of your choice and pay for it later—the same with the car, the furniture, the clothes, the jewelry. Instant coffee and frozen foods—all wonderfully efficient boons to modern living. But some things don't change. It takes time to become very good at something. Young stars in major sports who are paid those astronomical salaries and bonuses have been playing those sports, and playing them exceedingly well, for many years. Mike Milken of the investment banking firm of Drexel Burnham is just thirty-nine years old, yet he earns many millions of dollars a year—$40 million in 1985*—a sum so staggering to the average mind, even to the mind of the upper-income person, that it's difficult to comprehend. Yet he earns it, or it would not be paid. He works eighteen hours a day, seven days a week at his job. He puts together billion-dollar buyouts. He is apparently a River Person and has found a very special, very fast, deep river. He has time for nothing else. He plays a piano with one key.

"Not for me," you and I say, and I think we're right. I want to spend time on the golf course and on my boat. I want to do some traveling, and I like to have the time to buy things, not just earn money. But when I work, I work hard, and I stay with and finish what I begin. Most of all, I want to spend time with Diana. I enjoy her company. I can't do all those things and work eighteen hours a day. I can do all I need to do in a good solid six hours a day, sitting at my typewriter and poking about in my research library. That often includes Saturday and Sunday. But it still leaves plenty of time for other interests.

There seems to be a door on the way to remarkable success that can be passed through only by those willing to persevere beyond the point where the majority stop and turn back. Few of us realize in the early days how long it takes to succeed in an extraordinary way. And it should take sufficient time. It is a process of preparation, testing, and retesting, a process of growth and education, so that when we do pass through that door into the interesting and gratifying realm beyond, we are qualified and bear the scars of repeated attempts. We are initiated, quite thoroughly.

* *Business Week*, July 7, 1986.

But time will pass anyway, whether we do or do not, so it makes sense to stay with it, to hang on for a while longer and get in the habit of surmounting challenges; there will be more of them up the road. Problems don't end with our first success. Problems are integral to living. Successful people are not people without problems—they are people who have learned to solve their problems.

As the distinguished actor John Houseman said in his TV commercials for Smith-Barney in the early Eighties, "They *earn* it." It's not only the old-fashioned way—it's the only way.

People say, "I need to make some money!" The only people who make money are people who work in the mint. They take very special paper, very special inks, and very special engraving, and they manufacture—actually make—money. That's how they earn their living. And like them, we must earn ours. And just as it would be better if, instead of saying, "I need a job," we said, "I must find a way of being of service," it would be a good idea to say, "I need to earn some money." It changes the entire attitude. Many do say it that way, and they succeed in earning the money they need.

Early in this chapter I talked about starting my own radio program on WGN Chicago and how difficult it was to sell time on the program in the beginning. Let me point out that in 1950 television was still rather new. It was so exciting and important a medium that for a long time it seriously overshadowed radio in the minds of the advertising community. Much the same thing happened when radio was invented. Everyone was saying, "Who'd buy a newspaper when you can get the news instantaneously and free just by owning a radio?" But newspapers still flourish, of course, and offer a great deal that isn't found on radio or television. Similarly, radio, the most ubiquitous and pervasive medium of them all, is alive and well. Radio stations have flourished and multiplied, and even if they were only listened to by the drivers of automobiles, they would still be a good advertising buy. But radio is much more than that. The quality of an advertisement determines its effect, and the same is true for radio stations.

Television is not "better than" radio by any means. I recall the years when I played the part of Sky King on radio. It was a highly rated network kid's show, and we regularly performed feats of derring-do on the radio program that would have been impossible in those days on television. I recall one episode in which I was fighting an arch-criminal on the wing of a jet airplane. We wore suction cups on our shoes, if my memory serves, and thanks to our talented sound-effects man, it sounded to millions of kids as if we were doing just that. As the jet sped through the air at high speed and at a considerable altitude, with sounds of the air roaring, the jet engine screaming, the loud suction cups plopping about, and the two combatants grunting, I was successful in vanquishing my wily foe. But not until Mike Wallace had interrupted to sell Peter Pan Peanut Butter. And sell it he did. At that time practically all television was live, and we found ourselves saying after the program, "Let them try that on television!"

And today, as I write these words, my syndicated daily radio commentary is heard on hundreds of radio stations throughout the United States, Canada, Mexico City, Australia, New Zealand, South Africa, the beautiful Bahamas, and many places in between. None of which would have happened if, years ago, I hadn't kept muttering "stay with it!" Just the other day I received a letter from our station in Guam inviting Diana and me to share Thanksgiving Day with them. Radio is not only alive and well—it is simply everywhere! My induction into the Radio Hall of Fame in the spring of 1986 was one of the real highlights of my life.

CHAPTER VIII

Making It on Your Own

Entrepreneur—en-tre-pre-neur (än'tra-pra-
nür') n. *A person who organizes, operates, and
assumes the risk for business ventures, especially
an impresario. The word comes from Old
French. See* enterprise.
American Heritage Dictionary

For entrepreneurs, America was, and is, truly a paradise. All business activities in the United States and its territories began as entrepreneurial adventures. Trace any corporation back to its beginnings, or to the beginnings of its parent corporation, or to the beginnings of *its* parent corporation, and you'll find it began as an idea that would fill, or help fill, a need or desire on the part of the human beings who would become the company's customers. Only human beings can buy things or order that they be bought, even if the things purchased are for the consumption of things not human, like chickens, hogs, or beef cattle.

We look today at a complex multinational organization like IBM and forget that the company began in the mind of a single human being. Anyone who starts, or causes to be started, a business venture is an entrepreneur. An impresario is one who does in the world of entertainment what an entrepreneur does in the world of business. Quite often the two are combined, for certain businesses are endlessly entertaining, for those deeply connected with them as well as for their customers. Both impresarios and

109

entrepreneurs need customers—without them they will quickly close, and their investments will go down the drain.

The entrepreneurial adventure is endlessly attractive to those endowed with entrepreneurial spirits—adventurers, in varying degrees, whose visions of the future tend to be sanguine rather than sanguinary, that is to say, hopeful and enthusiastic rather than defeatist. The entrepreneur is the person who says, "I think it will be a big success." The nonentrepreneur says, "You're going to lose your shirt!"

A survey of the most successful people in a large American city, taken many years ago, revealed that most of their ultimate success depended in large measure on the jobs they had lost. Whether they had resigned or been fired wasn't all that important. And under the questioning, these very successful people thought about that interesting fact perhaps for the first time, and they shuddered to think what their present lives might have been like had they clung to that early job that at the time seemed so important to them and their families.

They were not all entrepreneurs, of course, but they were people with faith in themselves and their ideas, which is the mark of success wherever it is found. During those important steps in their careers, they were no doubt warned by well-meaning relatives and friends to hang on to the jobs they had held, and they were no doubt lectured on the dark and dismal pitfalls of venturing off with something as ephemeral and evanescent as an idea! But of course good ideas are not ephemeral or evanescent, as some might fear. They are the most important things in our biosphere. And it is producing ideas that raises the human being to his or her highest levels of achievement. Ideas solve problems and make our lives infinitely more interesting and rewarding, less dangerous, better fed, better employed, richer in countless ways, and wonderfully more comfortable. Without ideas we would still be sitting in the trees grooming one another.

All creatures on the planet use life-saving techniques. Some are fleet of foot; others are sharp of claw and fang. There are fish in the deep dark trenches of the oceans that dangle tiny lanterns above their waiting jaws. But the human being has the brain, the idea-producer, to save his or her skin in myriad ways. And the United

States, the only nation on the planet with the word *happiness* in its official chartering papers, offers a number of options to those desiring to share in the good life. One of those options is the right to go into business with little more than an idea and the determination to succeed. In 1986 about 700,000 Americans did just that.

The idea that results in a person running the risks of starting his or her own business depends strictly on the person—the person's background, education, previous level of accomplishment, and aspirations.

For some it may mean opening an adult bookstore—a euphemism that irritates me no end, since in my view a bona fide adult wouldn't be caught dead in one. I use that example because I can't think of anything lower on the scale of human wants. And entrepreneurs serve human wants more than they do actual needs. I've received letters from radio listeners and customers of our audiocassette programs asking me how I justify the wealth and apparent success of people who make their money in various kinds of base pursuits. I remind my questioners of my favorite definition of success: "Success is the progressive realization of a worthy ideal or goal."

Success is available to all who will take charge of the direction of their lives and aim it toward ideas, ideals or goals that they feel to be worthy. And while you and I may not feel the dissemination of pornography to be worthy of us or worthy of anything at all, there are those who actually do, and they'll give you all sorts of arguments to bolster their belief. They are entrepreneurs in any case, since they do fit that definition.

I picked the worst example I could think of to show that the type of business a person begins is a reflection of that person's mind, the way he or she tends to think. For hundreds of thousands of financially successful people, how they make a profit is not nearly as important as the fact that the profit is produced. If they remain successful from a financial standpoint, they believe they know what they're doing. There is a steady market for their products and services, or they would go broke.

And human wants are as varied as human beings themselves. The mind-boggling success of the illegal drug business in America is a good example. I've seen reports that place the illicit drug trade ahead of tourism and citrus in Florida, making the sale and shipment of illegal drugs Florida's number-one industry. It does billions of dollars of business, on which not a dime of taxes is paid. Those profits go many places and wind up in many pockets of people who evidently feel that if you can get away with it and if people want it and will pay the high prices for it, it's good business.

But as we talk about pornographers and drug dealers and entrepreneurial activity, let's remember that word *worthy* in our definition of success. Do we feel it's a worthy business to be in? How about our kids, our wives? Do you want to live next door or across the street from a drug dealer or pornographer, or even in the same neighborhood?

Fortunately for all of us, the examples we've mentioned form only a ragged lunatic fringe about the main body of American entrepreneurial activity. For most of us, going into business is a perfectly honest pursuit, although beset by many problems, irritations, headaches, sleepless nights, long hours, and low pay. Ah, yes—being in business for oneself does not necessarily mean an inordinately high income. On the contrary, it often means very little or no income at all for long periods of time. But once the business hits, whether it takes five years or fifteen, you've got the world by the nether parts. You decide what you're worth in the salary and bonus departments, and the company can foot the bill for much that would ordinarily come out of an employee's pay. Becoming truly successful usually takes longer than we realize when we begin. Like the decision to have a child, we seldom take into consideration the length and arduous nature of the contract. But if our idea is sound, and if we are sound, and if we fully understand the concept of service and the importance of working capital and of constant upgrading of our products or service, and if we have the perseverance of a Columbus, we will wake one fine morning to find ourselves one of the competent ones of our generation. We will have achieved a kind of independence never known or understood by an employee, no matter how high he or she may travel in the hushed corridors of executive country.

America's top executives working for large multinational corporations usually earn more in salary and perks, stock options, and bonuses than the great majority of entrepreneurs. But the entrepreneur has something else: control. Once the business is truly successful, which means it is probably in a state of happy expansion, the entrepreneur can hire the best executives to run things while he or she takes a vacation in Hawaii or Gstaad, or plays golf in Nairobi, or does a bit of deep-sea fishing in the Saychelles.

"You say it might take fifteen years for that kind of success?"

Yes, I do. But how long would it take you if you worked for Beatrice Foods or Chrysler?

"Fifteen or twenty years I suppose, if ever."

Right!

And the fifteen years or whatever time it takes aren't all pain, suffering, and sleepless nights. There's a lot of joy in there, too. There's the joy of seeing your own ideas in action and of watching your own ideas and efforts win against the competition. There's the joy of watching money pour in along with the orders. There's a sort of kindly vindication in that.

When I resigned from CBS, my friends told me repeatedly what an idiot I was. They reminded me that there were ten thousand guys in the United States who would part with one of their gonads for my contract with CBS. I had reached the top. I went to work in the world-famous Wrigley Building in Chicago, beautifully paneled, brass-trimmed elevators. I rubbed shoulders with the rich and famous, and I earned top dollar in my profession. Thousands—no, millions—listened when I read the news or the latest Jell-O commercial. Man! I was on top of the heap! I had it made, and I was only twenty-eight years old!

It does little good to remonstrate with an entrepreneur. Christopher Columbus, brilliant navigator that he was, could have spent his life in peace navigating up and down the coastal waters of Europe, remaining within the known boundaries of the period's world maps. But at the edges of the known waters there appeared the terrifying legend, "Here there be dragons!" And it was there that Columbus desired to sail. And it is there that every entrepreneur desires to sail.

It's interesting to note that on the old maps beyond the known world, there was never a legend reading, "Here there be unlimited opportunity for exploration. No doubt much gold and silver and precious gems. Strange human creatures live beyond these boundaries, waiting for discovery and development for the daring and intrepid sailor." Even though it had always been that way in the known world, no one ever suggested that it might still be that way in remaining undiscovered areas. It was the natural proclivity of cartographers and is still the tendency of advice-givers to look upon the unknown as bad. Like children going into a darkened basement alone, they feel that the dark and the unknown must hold strange and fearful creatures unimaginable in the known and lighted world. They cannot think otherwise; it is their nature, as it is the nature of bankers, CPAs, many wives, many husbands and all brothers-in-law. "What a dumb idea!" they say. At the time of Columbus, not a single live dragon had ever been seen on the earth by anyone. Dragons were, in fact, fairy-tale creatures. Yet they always inhabited the uncharted regions of the world. It said so right on the maps.

So when you get an idea that you think will result in an excellent business of your own—and it needn't be a new idea, by any means—keep it to yourself and your secret note pad for a period of time while you simmer it on the rotisserie of your minds—conscious and unconscious. Let it turn while you view it from every angle. Look at it from the standpoint of the worst possible scenario. If it's a good, sound idea, it should survive even the worst times, as good businesses do. Incidentally, there are recession-free businesses; many businesses do as well or better in recessions than in good times.

It was during the very worst years of the Great Depression that the American film industry really got it together. Delightful taffy merchants in uniform wore white cotton gloves in front of the better Los Angeles theaters; what wonderful hard taffy that was, and what opulent, magnificent palaces were the motion–picture theaters of that time! For the American poor they took the place of the great Gothic cathedrals of the Middle Ages. All that, and free dishes to boot! And the Saturday–morning matinees—what cliffhangers! Remember Harold Lloyd on the face of that great clock? All for a dime, although older folks had to pay fifteen cents.

And there was Wrigley's chewing gum—which got its start as a premium in boxes of soap!—and miniature golf, Monopoly, the hamburger stand, and radio. What a time for the entrepreneur! Despite the worst doldrums the nation had ever experienced from a fiscal standpoint, it was the very time that saw the beginnings of thousands of companies that are today among the giants of the world. And there were many, despite the options, that failed ever to appear again. All those auto companies, for example. We had a Pierce Arrow at one time, and a Reo Flying Cloud. All are now in the big garage in the sky.

So what's your bag?

Unfortunately, the decision to become an entrepreneur, like the decision to marry, does not at the same time confer upon the person making the decision a sudden burst of improvement in the intelligence department. The person who has spent his or her life up to the time of decision in the assiduous avoidance of useful information will discover the same difficulty in further success that he or she has no doubt met with in the past. Entrepreneurial activity is not an escape from discipline. It is, in fact, the exact opposite. If you're a creative genius with little affection or aptitude for keeping books, for example, make sure you have a partner you both trust and know to be competent in the areas of your incompetence. Or be able to contract for such services, the very best you can find. And make a regular examination of the books part of your regimen, no matter how dull or uninteresting you may find it. Ignorance is, unfortunately, no excuse for failure. You can learn to read a financial statement and assess your accounts receivable even if your hair grows to your shoulders.

I commented at the beginning of this section that for entrepreneurs America has always been a paradise. To thousands of worried, harried, struggling entrepreneurs, the word *paradise* will no doubt bring a wry smile or perhaps one of the earthly expletives commonly heard on the docks.

"I should have kept my job!" many will say. "Now I'm $150,000 in debt, with my house, car, and dog in hock and my wife and mother-in-law giving me hell every time I manage to get home. Some paradise!"

For thousands of once-hopeful companies, Chapter 11 bankruptcy seems like the only way out: reorganization for the benefit of creditors, and not much benefit at that.

"You've got to be a foreign country in the American defense perimeter to be guaranteed any kind of security." I've heard all the comments and at times have muttered a few myself. There are no guarantees. Don't confuse opportunity with guarantee. And it's best that you get rid of that terrible word *security* now, once and for all. There is no such thing as security as long as you're alive. Dead, you're secure. Unborn, you're secure. If you're alive, you are the very epitome of insecurity. Think about it: You're on a small planet hurtling through space—the mystery of space—at about one million miles an hour. The dinosaurs were here for nine million years and were far more successful as living creatures than we've been with our short-lived appearance as Johnny-come-latelys. And they were extinguished in a matter of weeks because of a giant meteor that raised so much dust it obliterated the sun, and they froze to death.

Security! There's no such thing. There's opportunity. There's joy. There's love. There are all kinds of wonderful things to do and see and experience, but there's no security whatever. Can you call an eighty-year existence in the billions of years the universe has been around security? Okay, eighty-five or so. The kind of security most people are looking for—that's their home and car that the bank has as collateral for their loans. They can be resold.

So you have to ask yourself—or at least it's a good idea to ask yourself— "What do I want to do with my time, however short or long it may be? Do I want to make it big? Do I want to see the world and live in penthouse apartments overlooking the sea and drive fine European cars and command a fifty-foot flybridge sport fisherman with twin diesels throbbing below my feet? Or do I want to make a difference with what I believe to be a very good idea or talent that I have worked very hard to hone to marketability? If the money comes, great, I can spend it as well as the next guy. But I'm happiest doing my thing, and I don't want a boss telling me what to do for the rest of my working life. I want to be independent as much as that's possible, considering I can only succeed to the extent that I serve others. My public, whatever that amounts to, is my boss. I must please those people, or they won't give me the money to buy the things I need and want."

Elementary, my dear Watson.

"But if we have just that little time to live, who would want to spend it, as you say, 'tiptoeing through life trying to make it safely to death'?"

Lots of people. Short time, long time—most people get very nervous when they think of being in charge of their own economic well-being. They want that check every week. The one with that great name at the top that makes everyone glad to cash it. And don't knock it. That's what your own key people will be like. If they were all in business for themselves, there'd be a lot more competition than there is. And keep in mind that competition only exists if you choose to play Follow the Leader. Rolls-Royce isn't in competition with anyone; nor is Mercedes-Benz, really. Take a look at IBM and the rest of the top cats: people at the top of their lines of business. Nope, they're not too concerned about competition, either, they're too busy creating. If you're a pacesetter, you're not competing, you're leading, you're creating! You've carved your own niche out of the market, like Poggenpohl Kitchens or Baker furniture.

My company doesn't have any competitors. We have copiers and followers, sure; that's the sincerest form of flattery. But competitors? No. We never will have them, as long as we have the creative management we've got and the team that puts it all together. You won't see us on *Fortune's* list of the top 500 corporations in America. But we're number one in our industry. We founded the industry. And after twenty-seven years, we still look upon it as a fledgling, just getting its flying feathers.

Pie in the sky? People have been telling people like us that all our lives. Do you know what pie in the sky really is? It's the vision of a piece of pie a truck driver gets as he approaches the truck stop. It's pie in the sky only for a short while. Then there it is on the counter, dripping with sweet juice and apples oozing out. "Helen, how about putting a scoop of vanilla ice cream right there on top? Thanks. Mmm! That's good!" That was pie in the sky; now, *urp!* it's a delicious memory.

We tend to make our delicious visions real in our lives. That most of us downscale our visions into the easy-to-accomplish variety is a fact of life. Most of the time, we're not even aware that the process of getting a strong vision and then making it come true is in operation. And we seldom give much thought, if any at all, to the fact that if the process will work for a piece of apple pie, it may work for anything.

When they go into business, the great majority of entrepreneurs make the same mistake that most people make just living their daily lives—they unconsciously play Follow-the-Leader. There is an unspoken, unmentioned, perhaps unthought–about assumption that whatever people in great numbers are doing must be the right thing to do. Why? The great majority of people do not achieve unusual success; why would we expect that getting in the same line with them in any endeavor would result in any sort of remarkable success? We tend not to think about it. "If all the motels look like that, or at least most of them, I guess it's okay to build mine to look like that." "If all the other hardware stores I've seen look like that one over there, and I want to go into the hardware business, I guess it's okay to make my store look like that, also." Or drugstore, or beauty salon, or real–estate office, or barbershop, or grocery store, or supermarket, or electronics store. By looking, that is to say, by appearing to be no different from all the other people in that line of business, I can see to it that I am competing with all the others, who of course have a head start on me.

That's why the fast-food chains—McDonald's, Burger King, Wendy's, and the rest—have been successful. Nobody in the small towns and neighborhoods in which they're located had the brains or creative talent to start an independent operation that was as fetching and efficient. I know that because I drove my car from southwest Florida all the way to Carmel, California, without seeing a single independent fast-food operation with a sign reading, "If we can't serve you better, more delicious food than the big fast-food chains, we'll pick up your check."

"Hey, don't try to buck the big boys" goes the myth. And myth it is. The fact is that a local, well–managed operation can beat a national chain operation hands down every time. And "local" can grow to "regional," and it can still whip the pants off the national operation. It can be built into a fine, very substantial business and then be sold for a ton of money or gradually be expanded into a national organization.

I can remember when people were saying, "Hey, wait a minute. You're not going to compete against Hilton Hotels, are you?" Dozens have, and most of them are waxing fat and prosperous.

The point I'm making here is that you don't have to pioneer a brand-new industry, the way Lloyd Conant and I did in electronic/audio publishing. Or the way our good friends Wallace Johnson and Kemmons Wilson did with Holiday Inns.

You don't have to pioneer a new industry if you don't want to, although there's fun and profit in that if you can stay the distance. Instead you can go into an old, well-established business and just do it a bit better in a more interesting way. And that applies to any business. There isn't one that's being done as well as it could be. The best ad has still to be written, although there are some mighty good ones out there. It's all a matter of how hard you want to work, for how long.

I don't know how many American entrepreneurs could be called wonderfully successful, or even what percentage. It's a small percentage, I'm sure. Most of them, as I said, are still playing copycat with each other. They join associations and attend conventions and conferences to find out what the more successful among them are doing, but it's still largely a game of playing copycat. Here and there the creative independent makes it big.

One time I was having breakfast at a small village café in Punta Gorda, Florida, a small town on the southwest coast of Florida, about fifty miles south of Sarasota and twenty miles or so north of Fort Myers. It's an old town in which you can still hear the crackers crunching on the still nights. There are lots of old homes, many with tin corrugated roofs, and there are brick streets. It wasn't much of a café; it was exactly like a zillion others throughout the South. But on this particular morning, the owner asked if he could sit with me with a cup of coffee. I'd finished breakfast, so I told him it was all right, although his chain smoking irritated me.

He said, "Could you tell me what I could do to increase my

breakfast business?" And since I'd seen his menu and had a good look at his clientele, I said, "Yes, I can tell you how to substantially increase your breakfast business."

"How's that?" he asked with all the insouciance of a man used to getting free advice.

"Start serving country ham with eggs, grits, big homemade baking-powder buttermilk biscuits, and red-eye gravy."

He looked at me silently, his eyes in their perpetual squint through the cigarette smoke. And then he said, "My cook would never stand for that. She'd never agree to it in a thousand years!"

So I said, "If your cook is in charge of this place, why are you asking me what you could do to improve your breakfast business?"

He smiled and shook his head and went back to his cash register, mumbling, "Nope, she'd never agree to that in a hundred years."

I had never seen his cook. Perhaps she was also his mother-in-law. Whoever she was, she had him buffaloed, and apparently she decided what would and would not be served in the place. He never asked my advice again. He's still there, eking out a living. But because I liked living there for a while, and because there was no decent place to eat, I got my friend Don Donelson to join me on a venture. We built a fine restaurant on an old, ruined, tumbledown pier that we restored. The restaurant is still there in a beautiful setting with a marina and a harbor view that's second to none in the state of Florida. In case you're ever in the neighborhood, drop in for lunch or dinner. Ride the glass-walled elevator up to Earl Nightingale's Restaurant. I think you'll like it. While you dine, you can watch the yachts coming and going and perhaps see a porpoise or two. The sunsets will bring tears to your eyes.

There is an organization in Hurst, Texas—part of the Dallas–Fort Worth metroplex, as they call it—named the National Association for the Self-Employed. They have told me that there are about twelve million self-employed people in the United States. Are self-employed people entrepreneurs? Not necessarily. If the definition of an entrepreneur is a person who organizes, operates, and assumes the risk for business ventures, the many thousands of physicians, dentists, CPAs and attorneys are not entrepreneurs. Some of them are, but most are not. They are simply self-employed professionals in business to practice their specialty. Some are wonderfully successful, most earn a pretty good living, some have a hard time.

For the purposes of the NASE, a self-employed person is one who has five or fewer employees, as a doctor might, or a small attorney's office. It also includes people in real estate, financial planners, insurance people, and the keepers of small shops, barbers and hairstylists and all the rest. Shopkeepers are entrepreneurs, whether they act the part or not. There's a well-known story about a shopkeeper in the Bronx who was struck by a car one day and knocked down. The police officer for the area, who knew the man well, rushed to his aid, put his own coat over the man's prostrate form, and asked, "Mr. Steinberg, are you comfortable?" Mr. Steinberg gave the question a little thought and replied, "No, I'm not comfortable, but I make a good living."

I think Mr. Steinberg typifies the American shopkeeper. Quite often the shop is much more than a place in which one finds his "good living." It is often a place where one finds his very being, where he spends the day chatting with old friends and neighbors as he serves their needs. Where he can complain about the weather and the dismal plight of the Mets or the Kansas City Royals or the San Francisco Giants. It's a place where he interfaces with the people of his world, the people who give him his identity and *raison d'être*—his very reason for being. Quite often retirement is something he or she would rather not think about. There are no burning desires or impetuous goals tugging at the mind of this person. He or she makes a good living, pays taxes on whatever share of the income he or she feels is fair, votes in the local and national elections and tries to stay healthy.

And there's nothing wrong with that. Nothing at all. Delicatessen, convenience store, newsstand, cards and notions, stationery and office supplies—whatever the business, it works. And it's an option for us all. Such businesses come up for sale regularly in cities and towns across the country as their owners die or are forced by ill health or infirmity or whatever reason to sell out. They are well established and sufficiently profitable for a family to earn a satisfactory living. It's a matter, as it is with most people, of fitting the living standard to the income.

But it is also quite possible, and also an option, to fit the income to the living standard. Once one decides how he or she wants to live and what it will take in the way of income to live like that, one has a goal, an income goal, to reach. And for such people America is also a paradise, because in America—as in many Western democracies and now in the Pacific Basin—the sky is no longer the limit in the income department. The income is only tied to what one does to earn it in the way of providing services or products for customers. But for those who wish to climb into the higher realms of income, perhaps membership in the National Association for the Self-Employed won't cut it.

And it is here that the entrepreneur really comes into his or her own.

As I said earlier, all of us come from humble beginnings if we go back far enough, and most of us don't have to go back very far. Quite often twenty or thirty years will do quite nicely. But if you are to move from a quite average income into the realms of higher income—that is, to fit your income to your lifestyle goals, with your lifestyle goals in the upper brackets—you are going to have to make some internal adjustments first.

First you must know that the pathway is open to you. You must believe that there are no artificial barriers, such as class restrictions, to your climbing all the way to the very top if that is what you desire. And there are not.

You must then adopt, practice, and make a daily part of yourself an attitude of cheerful expectancy. You must *know* that the success you are beginning to dream about will be yours, that it is only a matter of time, that you are leaving the ways of your family, neighbors, relatives, school chums, and acquaintances and climbing into the rarefied realms of achievement and wealth. You know it will take time, but the time will pass anyway, whether you climb out of the average way of life or not. You need to know that you must acquire an education of a sort that will qualify you to find your place in those loftier realms of achievement and wealth. And you need to know that since you will become what you think about, you've got to stop thinking in ordinary ways. The success you seek is not ordinary; it is extraordinary, and you must begin immediately to think in extraordinary ways.

You need to begin asking yourself, "How can I be of unusual service to enough people that my commission on that service will add up to the lifestyle that I have chosen for myself?" All entrepreneurs in business for themselves, as heads of their own enterprises, are, in the final sense, on straight commission. They can take no more from the business than their fair share. If their fair share comes to $300,000 a year, that enterprise must either serve a great many people or sell a very high-ticket product.

For example, if you sell someone a yacht for $600,000, your commission on that sale might come to $30,000. You will need ten such sales to earn your $300,000. Or you can make a product on which you earn a dollar apiece and sell the product to 300,000 people. That's less than the total population of a good-size American city. Either will do. And if you can double your sales in either case, you can earn $600,000 a year, or half the salary of a top NFL quarterback.

At least you're starting to think along lines that no one in your family, since its founders put down their stone axes and took up a plow, has ever thought along before. And as you do, your inner culture is undergoing a significant change. The cutting away from the average has to begin, as everything has to begin, in the mind, and from the mind to the attitude, then back into the mind until it's all a piece and the ideas start to come.

Interestingly, this is not the way most entrepreneurs start things. They usually get started in an attempt to prove a point, to prove they know what they're talking about and thinking about. Quite often an entrepreneur begins as an employee pleading with his boss to take a new tack. The boss shakes his head like the repository of all wisdom he often believes himself to be and says, "No, it'll never work." Whereupon the burgeoning entrepreneur says, "It will work. It's a good idea. It will revolutionize this business, and I'm going to do it. I quit."

It seldom happens that quickly. There may be months of agonizing, long talks into the wee hours of the morning with the spouse, serious discussions with friends, even a few sorties into the possibility of raising money on the outside before the final decision is made. But dozens of the most successful companies in the world began in the mind of an employee who had to quit and start his own business to prove he was right. Quite often he had no lifestyle goals to shoot at, just a burning desire to do what he had tried unsuccessfully to get his boss to let him do within the framework of the organization he worked for. One day a smiling accountant shows him his company's profit picture, and he realizes he's rich and that he and the family can move out of the old place with the hole in the living-room carpet and the one-car garage into something nicer, which will more accurately represent his true place in the community. That usually takes fifteen to twenty years to happen, but in this new age we've stumbled into, it often happens in a lot less time than that.

But all of this makes the entrepreneur a different kind of cat. The fact that he got the idea for the change in the first place sets him apart. Everyone else is usually quite content to go along as before without thinking about anything at all, even their boss. The fact that he became so involved with the idea also sets him apart; he's a person with the courage of his convictions, to use an overworn cliché. He believes so firmly that he is right, he's willing to stake his job security on the idea and go it alone. That makes him quite different. If he'd been employed by 3M or some other change-oriented company, it would have financed his idea within the company, given him the people he needed, and told him to go ahead, make it work. And if it did become all that he thought it would become, he would be as well rewarded within the old organization as he might have become as head of his own company on the outside. He would have become an *intrapreneur*, and he could go from one success to another, all within the supportive framework of a major multinational corporation. He would have access to millions of dollars' worth of equipment, including the latest computers, first-class people, an existing plant, and unlimited financial backing. It all depends on the outfit you are working for to begin with.

But if you want to make it on your own, in your own organization—and most entrepreneurs do—then you must become a people person. You have two audiences that must like you and feel you have their interests at heart: your customers and prospects, and your employees.

I'm a longtime *Forbes* magazine fan. I think it's the best business publication to read. In the *Forbes* issue of December 3, 1984, there was a very interesting story in the Psychology and Investing section by Srully Blotnick. (What a wonderful name. It has to be his real name, because he could never have dreamed it up in a hundred years. It's much better than a pen name. It's unforgettable.) The piece was titled, "People Do Matter." It was about young people fresh from business school going into business in great numbers. One young man had to file for bankruptcy after three and a half years, even though all the right numbers were there. Everything had been by the book, just the way they'd taught at the best business schools in the country, except for one thing: The business schools had forgotten about people, the way they tend to do in the ivory towers of academe. People make all the difference in the world, and if they're not with you, you go out of business. It's people you're serving, and it's people you depend on for part of the money they earn each month. They'll happily share it with you if you give them good service, if they feel important in your place of business. They don't care about the business–school numbers. They're like flowers; they turn their faces and open their wallets and purses to the radiance of people who love and respect them enough to do business their way.

Now it's true that if you have a hot–dog stand in the middle of Grand Central Station in New York City, you'll do a good business whether you're nice to people or not. In fact, in New York City there are a number of businesses that do quite well and barely acknowledge the customer at all. The Plaza is such a place. Unless you're a well-known celebrity, forget it. You'll wait your turn, and then you'll wait a little after that, until it pleases the waiter or captain to acknowledge your presence; after one visit, that may be it for the day. My wife and I waited for our waiter at breakfast one morning until we were afraid they were going to start switching over to the luncheon menus. Finally capturing the attention of a young woman who worked there, we inquired if she would ask our waiter to come to our table, whereupon she snapped, "He's busy right now!"

He wasn't busy waiting on tables; that was obvious. We wondered at what he might be busy. Perhaps he had a hobby he practiced in the butler's pantry or was moonlighting at some other job. But getting breakfast at the Plaza, like getting anything else, is a pain in the acetabulum. We received a thousand percent better service the following week at the Sheraton Hotel in Billings, Montana, where I had a date to make a speech. But there aren't millions and millions of people in Billings, Montana. If one customer walks out in disgust in New York City, there are millions waiting to take his or her place who are quite willing to accept an unusually long wait along with cursory, hit-or-miss service and quite ordinary food at an outrageous price; many wouldn't know any other system. That's News York, except at 21 and Sardi's and a few other places where the service is as good as the food. You can only get away with that sort of thing after you're well established as a kind of institution. And the really great places, like Joe's Stone Crab Restaurant in Miami Beach, also give you great service along with great food—after you've waited an hour for a table. But I'm getting into the realm of my favorite nonwork pastime—good restaurants.

People will make you rich or keep you broke, depending on the way you serve them. You should make up your mind at the outset, if you're planning to become a successful entrepreneur, that you're going to make people—outside the organization and inside the organization—your special concern. As Srully Blotnick says, "People make the difference." They should teach that at the university business schools. Srully Blotnick knows what he's writing about. So does *Forbes* magazine. I think all entrepreneurs should subscribe to *Forbes*.

We have a no-questions money-back guarantee on all of our products at my company. Some years ago we received back in the mail a copy of my original recording, *The Strangest Secret*, in the old ten-inch jacket. It looked like a refugee from a Balkan war. In fact, it looked like it might have been dragged behind a horse. In the accompanying letter, the man said he was returning the recording and wanted his money back. We immediately cut a check and mailed it to him, along with our newest company brochure displaying all the new products we have produced. We got a letter back by return mail marveling at our honoring his request for a refund for a product that had so obviously been used up; he also sent a sizable order for several other products.

You can't lose money on a customer if you treat him or her the way he or she should be treated. Marshall Field used to receive a lot of kidding because of his policy of allowing merchandise to be returned if not completely satisfactory to the buyer. Women used to pretend to buy expensive fur coats, wear them for an important occasion, then return them for full credit the following day. But when kidded about such an occurence, Marshall Field used to request that the woman's account be sent up. Without fail, the woman was a regular customer who bought many other things on her account. She was a good customer. If she wanted to borrow a mink coat for an evening, so what? Chances are she'd talk her husband into buying one for her eventually. If not, she was still a good customer. It was his treatment of the customer that was largely responsible for Marshall Field's outstanding success. It's the same story at Neiman–Marcus, I. Magnin's and many others. The customer is queen or king, as the case may be.

There is never any excuse on the part of management for a customer being mistreated in any way. It simply shows a lack of training. And the lack of training of employees is one of the greatest problems of American business.

The other morning I had breakfast at Denny's Restaurant in Monterey. Denny's, incidentally, is quite a success story. The breakfast was fine, although the pancakes were a bit undercooked. But when I went to pay my check at the cash register, the attractive Oriental woman who took my money and gave me my change made no comment, nor gave me any sign of recognition. Recognition, that is, as a paying customer. In this case I leaned over the counter, smiled, and with a conspiratorial stage whisper I said, "You're supposed to say thank you."

Her face broke into a big smile, and she said, "Thank you," whereupon I said, "You're welcome!"

Not giving recognition to the customer is the worst offense anyone in business can commit. Recognition is number one on the hierarchy of human wants. Recognition is number one, stimulation or change is number two, and security is number three. The good businessperson and every one of his employees, because of their training, can give the customer all three.

The customer should be recognized, if at all possible, when he or she comes into the place of business. If customers have to wait in line, special attention should be given to them. Even a glance and the words, "I'll be with you as soon as I can," give the required recognition. And no customer should ever leave a gas station, convenience store, restaurant, or any other sort of business where other human creatures are involved in any way without special attention being given to thanking the customer. Even a good automated teller at a bank or savings and loan can say thank you, even if it only appears on the monitor screen. *Thank you for doing business with us.* It's recognition. As to stimulation and change, that's another side of good management. The business should never be permitted to settle down into a well-worn groove of sameness. Even little changes can make a big difference. Change is a sign of life, of interest on the part of management; it shows management cares about the customer. And security can be there, too. Good service is a kind of security, as is a fine product and a refund policy. Young people coming out of the public schools are not trained to handle customers. Everyone who works for us needs regular reminding that the customer needs to be looked at with a smile and to be told that he or she is appreciated. The customer needs to be given special care and thanked for sharing his or her hard-earned income with our place of business.

Reminding is as important as initial training and regular inspection. It's so easy to fall back into bad habits. I've stood at a cash register waiting to pay my bill while a seventeen-year-old girl talked with her girlfriend on the telephone. I waited five minutes and then simply walked out, got in my car, and drove away; she was still talking to her girlfriend on the phone. Customers should not wait to pay their checks, not a moment longer than absolutely necessary. Restaurant customers should never have to sit and wait for their checks to be delivered to the table. Customers are not supposed to be waiters; don't make them wait. Give them their checks before they're through dining, greet them with a smile at the cash register, and thank them—really thank them—and look at them when they pay their check. It makes them feel important to you, and of course they are important to you. They'll put you out of business if you don't give them the recognition they need. It's all so easy, really—all we have to do is treat customers the way we ourselves like to be treated. Never underestimate the customer—she's your wife. There are no unimportant customers, simply because there are no unimportant people. They want three things in this order: recognition, stimulation or change, and security. You can give them all three. And if you're wise, you'll never fail to give them all three.

The entrepreneurial opportunity is always there for those of us willing and eager to accept the risks and pay the price. It's well worth it. "If at first you don't succeed, try, try again."

CHAPTER IX

Happiness Is Saying "Yes"

There seems to be an ancient predisposition in the human race to say no. It is, of course, a conservative response—a status quo protector, a reactionary response that says, "I'm managing to cope with things as they are. Don't rock the boat—don't introduce any new problems for me."

Change of any kind always carries with it the possibility of change for the worse. We were reminded by Eric Hoffer in *The True Believer* that there is a conservatism of the very poor as rigid as that of the very rich. For the poor are managing survival. No matter how bleak their circumstances, they feel that any change may be for the worse. The very rich are quite content with things as they are, and they try very hard to keep them that way.

We all come from poor backgrounds, some more recently than others. The ancient fear of making a decision that could result in disaster still haunts our minds. However, successful people tend to say yes to life and its possibilities. They go out toward life in cheerful expectation of happy results. They enjoy the risks of considered opportunity and adventure. They have found that with their expectations, zeal, and commitment, they tend to win. The occasional negative result is shrugged off as part of the game.

We really can't keep on saying no if we expect to succeed. Survival should not be the only option for a human being. It's fine for horses and cows; pigs and chickens seem to thrive on it. But for the man or woman, simply surviving is stultifying and the beginning of the long slide toward oblivion. Human beings require more. It is important that we enjoy our time here and make some sort of contribution to the welfare of others. All but bent and twisted psyches will go along with that—the lifetime takers who have failed to mature. Our joy comes from producing, giving, and creating.

Being happy seems to depend on the direction in which we're headed. Happiness depends, at any given time, on moving toward something we wish to bring about in our lives. We can feel it in the smallest things: We are actually slightly happier when we are going out to dinner than we are on the trip home after dinner. We are happier on Christmas morning than we are on Christmas afternoon. We are happier when we are moving toward a goal than after we have achieved it. Remember the line, "Be choosy therefore what you set your heart upon, for if you want it strongly enough—you'll get it." In fact, the letdown, the depression following the successful achievement of a long-sought goal in life has from time to time led to suicide.

One struggling writer, after years of unflagging attempts, finally wrote a successful Broadway play. He found himself with an income of thousands of dollars a week. But he mysteriously took his own life. "Why?" people asked. He had found himself with nowhere to go. Instead of enjoying his newfound success for a few months and giving himself time to think of another play to write, suddenly, in an agonizing fit of depression and perhaps with too much to drink, he ended his life.

We need an endless succession of goals. George Eastman, of Kodak fame, although a much older man, ended his life, saying, "I've seen everything and done everything."

He was mistaken, of course, and if he could have imagined the changes that would soon be wrought in the photographic industry, he might have had second thoughts.

Our goals should form a tessellation, a mosaic, expanding from a center. We should move from one success to another, putting each in its proper place and adding it to our enjoyment and the enjoyment of others.

Sir Edmund Hilary didn't jump off Mount Everest after reaching its summit. It was a high point in his life, of course, and it brought him worldwide fame and a knighthood. But he went on about his business after that. And most successful people do much the same in their own way. They have their own Everests to conquer, and they conquer them. Achieving goals means saying yes to life and to its options and opportunities.

In the summer of 1986, my company produced a videotape program with Walter Payton of the Chicago Bears. Many people say Payton is the greatest football player who ever lived. In the interview, he was asked, "Do you have to do more planning now than you did in the past?"

Payton replied, "When I started out, I knew where I wanted to go, and I knew what I had to do to get there. And I looked at my progress as to where I was each year, each game. And I said, 'Well, this is where I want to be in three years; this is where I want to be in six years.' That's the way I approached it.

"When I was a kid, I used my imagination to create situations. And it's the same way once you start out in business, where there are things you want to accomplish. Everyone, when he opens up a new business or starts off, the first thing he wants to do—the first thing that comes to his mind—is not 'I want to be a thousandaire' or 'a hundredaire.' He wants to be a millionaire. And once you earn that first million in whatever you're doing...well...you sort of painted a picture of earning that million in your mind. That means more to you than actually earning that million, because after you earn that first million, then you have to use the imagination or that creativity inside of you to push yourself, to make yourself strive for more. You say, 'Well, I earned the first million. What's left for me?' Then you want to do more.

"It's the same in any other thing...in football, in life," Payton went on to say. "Once you experience something that you've dreamed about and you've reached that high, then you want to go a little bit farther. And to do that, you paint a picture in your mind. And the picture you paint in your mind about achieving something, about doing something, believe me, is far better than actually accomplishing it."

Then the great Walter Payton said, "It's that way with me. Going over ten thousand yards, passing Jim Brown's record"— Payton has since passed fifteen thousand yards to establish a new world record— "scoring so many touchdowns, getting into the

Super Bowl—as I'm approaching these milestones, the picture that I paint in my head and the perfume and the cherry blossoms and the incense that go along with it—you can't put it into words. But when you actually do it, it's not the same; it's not as great as when it was in your head.

"So after you accomplish it, you can't linger. You can't stay with it. All of a sudden you start to paint another picture; you set another goal for yourself, something to shoot for."

That's right, Walter Payton. You know, don't you? When you actually do it, it's not the same; it's not as great as when it was in your head. So you can't linger too long, can you? We need to keep saying yes to life. Who knows the extent of our possible growth?

We all know no-sayers. Let us not join their lugubrious legions.

An event that occurred in the summer of 1985 still sticks in my memory. People who venture to South Florida in the summer and then complain about the heat need some kind of professional help, but the summer of 1985 was hotter than usual. New records were set again and again, and even the radio and television weather people complained. That was the summer that Diana and I bought and were engaged in completely renovating our new home in Naples, Florida. One morning in July we were involved in our separate work in Fort Myers and, except for coffee and tea, missed breakfast. As midday approached, we found we were ravenous and drove to a nearby restaurant for an early lunch before heading down to Naples. It was one of those record-breaking, eye-squinting, sizzling days without a cloud in sight. We parked the car in a nearby lot and hurried through the heat to the shade of the front doors of the restaurant. We read the sign: OPEN 11:30. I glanced at my watch and saw that it was 11:25. But at least we were in the shade. We could certainly wait there for five minutes. As we stood there, we saw a young woman approaching the double doors. We were both thinking, "Oh, good, she's going to let us in early." Instead, the young woman opened the door about three inches, fixed us with a baleful look, and snapped, "We don't open till eleven-thirty!" Whereupon she slammed the door in our faces.

Diana and I looked at each other in silence for a moment, then joined hands and walked away. About a half-block away we found a place called J.B. Winberie's. There was a sandwich board sign in front, on which had been chalked the day's specials and from which floated some brightly colored balloons. It was friendly and cool, and its doors were open. The lunch was delicious. We had made a serendipitous discovery—we had turned a sad encounter into a definite positive.

But I found it difficult to get the incident out of my mind. The young woman hostess at the first restaurant had failed. She had failed as an employee, especially as a hostess, but more important, she had failed as a woman—as a human being. She had lost a couple of customers for her employer; she had been unconscionably rude and completely out of line. We had not knocked on the door and were quite willing to wait the few minutes necessary. But worst of all, she had failed utterly as a human being. She had shouted no to an opportunity to succeed and grow. She had shouted no when she should have said yes.

Why had she not said, upon unlocking the door, "Hello! Come in. You must be baking out there in the heat. We're not officially open just yet, but at least you can be cool and comfortable and look at our menu while you wait."

Another option would have been to offer us a cool drink of some kind. Just water would have been wonderful. But instead she had closed the door, not just on Diana and me but on her own opportunity to join the successful human beings of the world. It was a short-lived inconvenience for us. For her it was a significant opportunity missed. She was a smaller person because of her attitude. She had trapped herself, as millions do every day, because of a lack of information, a lack of education that's as old as the ruins of Carthage and as new and fresh as a cool spring morning. This education tells us that if our personal doors are not open, we cannot move into new, unexplored and opportunity-filled adventure. We need to know, as a basic part of our being, that unless our doors and windows are open, little can come into our lives to charm and interest us. People are like ponds or lakes; they need a constant inflow and outflow if they are to remain healthy, clean, and teeming with life. If they are damned all around—no pun intended—there is nothing for them but endless stagnation.

Millions suffer from this latter condition, as did the rude

hostess in Fort Myers, Florida, that hot morning in July. In slamming the door on Diana and me, she was shouting to the world that hers was a closed system. She lives a secondhand, truncated life, taking her cues from the other airheads with whom she associates, aping their manners and morals, laughing at their jokes, dressing as they dress, arranging her hair as they arrange theirs. She is not a true person in her own right but rather a cypher, a puppet whose strings are in the hands of people who don't know any more than she does and who certainly do not demonstrate any capacity for leadership.

A half-dozen great ideas could revolutionize her life and her world for the better. Her eyes would brighten with meaning and direction, and she would find herself smiling and reaching out for an opportunity to be of service. Our appearance outside her door that blistering day just a few minutes before the official opening time would have represented an opportunity to fulfill herself as a hostess and as a woman. The door would have been thrown open, and her smile would have brightened the day for all three of us. Afterward, we would have thought of her and the place in a kindly way. We would all have been enriched by the encounter.

The other day I asked a sales clerk about a product I was considering.

"It's not bad," she said.

I asked if that was the store's criterion for stocking its merchandise—that it not be bad.

"How about good?" I asked her. "Or even great?"

She smiled and moved away, no doubt thinking, "Who needs this character?" I had asked the question lightly, with a friendly smile, but her lack of training and indoctrination into the store's philosophy of doing business—if it had one—were obvious. Especially when we are interfacing with lots of people every day, we need reminding of the great ideas that can so easily change and improve our lives and the lives of others from bleak or blah or so-so to abundant, fine, and beautiful.

As I thought about the impoverished restaurant hostess, I remembered and read once again the beautiful lines of Elinor Lenz and Barbara Myerhoff in their excellent book, *The Feminization of America:*

Woman's historic responsibility for protecting life has endowed her with a set of adaptive characteristics: a strong nurturing impulse that extends to all living things; a highly developed capacity for intimacy that fosters her need for relatedness; a tendency to integrate rather than separate; an ability to empathize; a predilection for egalitarian relationships together with a resistance to hierarchy; an attachment to the day-to-day process of sustaining life; a spirituality that transcends dogma and sectarianism; a scale of values that places individual growth and fulfillment above abstractions; and a preference for negotiation as a means of problem solving, which springs from her antipathy to violence.

These are the very qualities that are so desperately needed in today's increasingly divisive and dangerous world. They offer the possibility for the kind of humanizing, life-enhancing relationships that both men and women are seeking and that so often elude us in the impersonal, bureaucratic, self-aggrandizing, high-tech society of America in the 1980's.

To think of the adaptive characteristics that Lenz and Meyerhoff wrote about, the characteristics that make so many women great, and then to think of our hostess and her sisters all over America—we can visualize the yawning chasm that divides them.

How do we get our great ideas and the hostess together? The first mistake was apparently that the woman had not been properly trained. She had not been told that the principal function of a successful business is the winning and keeping of customers. She had never been taught to say yes to customers.

Stew Leonard of Norwalk, Connecticut, operator of the world's most successful dairy store, displays his company policy for all to see, employees and customers alike:

OUR POLICY:

RULE NO. 1. THE CUSTOMER IS ALWAYS RIGHT.

RULE NO. 2. IF THE CUSTOMER IS EVER WRONG, REREAD RULE NO. 1.

That's it. Now, how would one of Stew Leonard's employees have reacted if they saw two customers show up a few minutes before official opening time?

So how do we get a few great ideas and the hostess under discussion together? The training room.

When a person applies for a job or answers an ad, we must assume that he or she knows nothing at all about business success. We must also assume that he or she knows nothing at all about how *we* do business or about the great laws that help us succeed as persons. We must begin with the fundamentals and then ask the people involved for feedback as to what we have been talking about. We need to make sure they understand why these great ideas are so important and why they will always work for us. We need to help them see their work as an opportunity for personal growth and remind them that the reason we are here is to serve one another.

We need to remind them regularly of the hundreds of thousands of people who serve them every day—who make the shoes and clothes they wear, prepare the food they buy at the grocery store and the restaurant, generate their electricity, operate their telephone system, manufacture everything in their homes that they tend to take for granted, supply the water for their morning showers and coffee, and pick the coffee beans. From the rugs on their floors to the roofing material that shelters them, they are constantly served in myriad ways, and now, here at work, it's their turn to serve. It's their turn to succeed or fail as human beings. Let's see how good we can make it all; let's find enjoyment in our work. Enjoyment is contagious and is picked up by the customer. Customers find they like to come to our place of business; they like the ambience, the mood of happy service. They like to kid around with the management and employees, and they expect first-class service with a smile and a thank you.

Hiring people without training them is a mistake; it can be a very serious mistake. An untrained employee in the wrong place can drive customers away in droves. People coming to work for the first time, and often for the second, third, or fourth time, often have no conception whatever of what makes a business succeed or fail. They think their paychecks come from the company they work for, when in reality they come from the customers. A company, like the federal government, has very little money of its own. It would go broke very quickly without the steady input of the customers. People who work for us need to know who the boss really is, that it's the customer, and they should be trained to treat the customer in exactly the same way they would treat the president or chairman of

the board of the company—or the Queen of England. Our employees, when they first come to work, need to be told that
everything they will ever own—their homes, food, clothes, school-
ing for the children, their automobiles, their savings—all comes
from the often funny-looking customer who comes walking in.
They need to be reminded from time to time that there are no
unimportant customers. That gangly teenage kid is just as important as the well-dressed sophisticated woman, and he will continue
to be important as he grows up. People in sneakers and sweatshirts
are just as important as the woman in the full-length mink.

After our experience with that hostess at the restaurant in Fort
Myers, Florida—the kind of employee who could cost an employer
several hundred dollars a week in lost business—we asked ourselves,
"What person in our acquaintance represents the exact opposite?
Who do we know who would represent the perfect employee—the
gold-medal, five-star employee?"

We thought immediately of our friend Leo Buscaglia who
teaches Love at UCLA and who has written a number of books and
produced several cassette–tape programs on the subject. We re-
called the time we had dinner with him at a Vietnamese restaurant
in Chicago. He had hugged and warmed the hearts of at least a
dozen people that night, and the whole place had been cheered by
his ebullient good spirits. Leo would be the perfect maître d' except
that he would be punched in the nose by irate escorts resenting his
enthusiastic hugging of their lady friends. But, of course, then he
would hug them, too.

Then we thought of Wally Amos of Famous Amos chocolate
chip cookie fame. Not only is Wally a phenomenon as a human
being, he is also one of the country's most successful businessmen.
Our last visit with him and his family was at the Kahala Hilton in
Oahu, Hawaii. The occasion was the third birthday of their
beautiful little girl.

Wally Amos is ebullience personified. He bubbles over with
high spirits and enthusiasm; he leaps out of his chair when you
approach his table in a restaurant, all smiles and happy greetings.
His greetings quickly include a growing circle of surprised bystand-
ers. Wally Amos attacks his work, whatever it happens to be, with
the enthusiasm of a man in a harem after five years in solitary

confinement. No matter where you put Wally Amos in your organization—driving the delivery truck, working on the loading dock or in the mail room—within a surprisingly short time he will be one of the people running the place. It's not just his enthusiasm; it's his brains and willingness to tackle big jobs.

Born a poor kid in Tennessee, after the breakup of his family he was shipped to live with his Aunt Della in New York. Aunt Della was the one who introduced him to chocolate–chip cookies and showed him how to make them. He attended a vocational school and was trained as a cook, but he matriculated to the William Morris Agency, where he, in fact, started in the mail room. Before long, he was a talent agent, and a good one. He still cooked his chocolate–chip cookies at home and brought them in as treats for his friends in the office. One day one of them said, "Wally, these are much too good to waste on a few friends. You should produce these cookies commercially and sell them all over the country." The rest is history. Now the Amoses live in a beautiful home on the windward side of Oahu. Wally commutes all over the country, stopping long enough, happily, to produce audiocassette programs for my company in Chicago. He has also written a book, *Famous Amos, the Man Who Launched a Thousand Chips*. I called Wally Amos and asked him to send me some of his ideas about his success. Here is what he said:

"Thank you for inviting me to be a part of your book. I will now attempt to answer your question or to give you some thoughts on why I say yes to life. First of all, I have the understanding that the Universe just responds to my thoughts. The Universe responds to me, to my actions. So whatever I send to the Universe, the Universe sends that right back to me.

"So, knowing that to be the truth, I have attempted to be as positive in my life as I possibly can. I want only positive results in my life and I know that if I project positiveness, if I give positiveness, then that's how the Universe is going to respond. Life is just a mirror, and what you see out there, you must first see inside of you. So I just work on really letting my light shine on treating people the way I want to be treated. I think the Bible really sums it up; it says 'Do unto others as you would have them do unto you.' And I want people to be respectful of me, to love me, to be generous to me, to encourage me, to support me in all the things that I do.

"So, in order to get that, I feel I have to give it. So I'm trying to practice my belief system. Practice what I teach. And that's why I say yes to life. Because I want life to say yes to me. I often reflect on my life, my entire life, and my success with Famous Amos, and I know that the only reason I have been a success with Famous Amos is because I've never looked back. I've never had any regrets, I've never tried to live in the past. It's always trying to be here right now, trying to put as much positive energy into this second as I possibly can. Knowing that the answer is right now, the answer is not yesterday or tomorrow, it's this second. That has been my attitude since I first started Famous Amos.

"I'll try many things, and those that work, fine. But I don't ever dwell on my so-called success. Because if I do, then there will be no more. If I wallow in the success of right now, it doesn't leave an opening for more success to come into my life. So I will have success and accept it, be grateful for it and then move on to something else. Because just as I think you can't live in the past in the negative way, I don't think we can live in the past at all. Not even positively. So as things happen, I acknowledge them, I learn whatever lessons they have brought to me. I give thanks for them. I give thanks to God and I'm just grateful for everything that happens to me. And then I move on.

"There are no negative experiences in my life because I believe that inherent within every experience is a lesson. It's something that I needed to learn. And I don't think anything is good, bad, positive or negative until we say so. So I have established an attitude that tells me that everything that comes into my life is good. And everything that comes into my life comes to teach me a lesson. To strengthen me, to help me rise to a higher level of consciousness. And I've proven to myself, time and time again, that if I don't get the lesson the first time around, that experience will repeat itself in my life until I do get it. The form changes, perhaps, the people change, but the experience is always the same.

"I heard a minister from Calgary say that the Universe always says yes. The Universe says yes to whatever thoughts you give it. If you say to the Universe, 'Hey, I can open a store selling chocolate chip cookies,' the Universe will say, 'Yes you can.' And then the Universe will proceed to support you in your endeavor. And you will ultimately open a store selling chocolate–chip cookies. By the same token, if you say to the Universe, 'Oh, God, I don't know how to open a store selling chocolate–chip cookies—this is far more than I could ever accomplish.' Once again, the Universe says yes. You will not be able to open a store selling chocolate–chip cookies.

"The Universe says yes to whatever thoughts *you* project into it. Whatever thoughts you give to the Universe, it throws them right back to you. So, knowing that to be the absolute truth, it is really important to say yes. To say yes in a positive way to experiences that come your way. It has created joy and happiness in my life. Saying yes to life has enhanced my life tenfold. So I am constantly looking for more ways to say yes so that I can experience good in all areas of my life. I think that life is really, really spectacular. I see this life all around me and know that God created it all and that he created me and gave me the ability to appreciate it. And that's just what I'm doing right now and know that the best is yet to come."

The Wally Amoses of the world are very special. We can train our employees to emulate them. My company, the Nightingale-Conant Corporation of Chicago, has one of the finest production teams ever put together. Collected one by one mostly, over the thirty years of our corporate life, they now number over two hundred and have a spirit seldom found in modern companies. Most of that is due to my late partner, Lloyd Conant, someone who said yes to life, who had a magical touch with people and knew that one of the best ways to let employees know they're appreciated is to pay them top dollar for what they do. He also knew—long before Tom Peters reminded the rest of the business community—the importance of MBWA, Management by Walking Around. Lloyd was often out in the plant talking to the printers, to the women in the shipping and billing departments, to everybody! He would rest a hand on their shoulder and, tell them what a great job they were doing and how proud he was of the team they'd put together. Once in a while we would get a large press of orders requiring our people to come in over the weekend. They never failed us, and Lloyd would make a party of it, with extra bonuses at Christmas time and a big dinner at a local restaurant at the time the extra work was performed.

While I don't think he ever articulated the idea, Lloyd knew we had two publics to be concerned about: first, the customer, and second, the employees. The business exists for the customers, so they must come first in everyone's mind; without the employees, nothing would happen.

Good management reaches the fineness of people and brings it to the surface. People want to help; they want to commit themselves in a good cause. When they find that management is on their side and an integral part of the whole team, they bring the best that's in them to their work. It becomes *their* company, *their* business, *their* customers. They are also aware that when they are asked to give up a weekend in the interest of getting the orders out, management is right there with them, working just as hard as they are. It's a team effort. Employees are always willing to say yes to good management.

There are no private parking spaces at our company, no executive bathrooms, no executive lunchrooms. Our company says yes to the world, and the world has been saying yes to us on a delightfully ascending scale for nearly three decades.

On the subject of saying yes to life, there are those who will say, quite properly, that there are times to say no. I agree. Living in the world of today and living well is a matter of choosing only a few special things from the torrent. That amounts to saying no to about ninety-nine percent of the things that clamor for our attention and money. On the other hand, the eclectic life is a matter of saying yes to those things and conditions that add to the quality, interest, and challenge of our lives.

I would like to touch again on the importance of training sessions for employees, especially new employees, but older ones as well. When you talk to them about the great ideas and laws that result in steadily growing success—as persons and as businesses—do not assume they fully understand the ideas you're sharing with them. Most people are not good listeners, and you may be talking to people who have been deeply conditioned to think in terms one hundred and eighty degrees from the points you are trying to make. To make certain they do know what you're saying and that they have fully assimilated the ideas, ask them to tell you what they understand you've been talking about.

Whenever he gave instructions on an important job to an employee, my partner Lloyd Conant would afterward ask the employee to tell him what he or she understood his or her instructions to be. The difference was often astonishing. So he would go over the instructions again, item by item, until he was sure the employee completely understood. That's important in teaching.

When steel–company employees were being laid off by the thousands, few of those let go fully understood the reasons behind their dismissal. They talked in terms of betrayal, as if the company could have kept them on if it had wanted to. When employees realize that their paychecks are written by the customers, they tend to take a different attitude toward their work. They see themselves not as workers for the company but as servers of the customers, and their work takes on new importance. It also becomes clear to them why companies need to constantly upgrade themselves technologically, even if it means shifting people around into different work. As long as they understand that increased efficiency means more customers and more business, they will feel relatively secure in their position with the company.

We need to say to our employees, "Our primary function is to win and keep customers. Thus we must grow more efficient and find new and better ways of being of service. We want and need your help in this effort. We want you to become an important and integral part of our corporate family. The better you get at what you do, the better this company becomes. Nothing we do now is as good as we hope to make it in the near future. Nothing is set in concrete. There are no set ways of doing things around here. If someone says to you, 'This is the way we've always done it around here,' question him. Why aren't we doing it in a better way? Maybe you can come up with a better way."

I have always thought it a good idea to share books with key people in the organization. Being a book lover myself, perhaps I'm a bit too conscious of the collections of books—or the absence of one of others. I think every executive with a future should have a good collection of important books. Or perhaps he or she is trying to stretch a degree, earned many years ago, much too far.

We teach our small children to say no to the stranger who offers them a ride in his car. We teach our children to say no to many things, and we say no to them quite properly. We say no to all that is demeaning and hurtful. When we learned that tobacco causes cancer and heart disease, we said no to tobacco. We say no to pornography and drugs, to all that is calculated to drag us down and make us less than we can be.

It has always been a point of interest to me that people take drugs and other so-called mind-expanding chemicals. The world and what it offers are sufficiently mind-expanding for me. The spectrum of options, stretching like a rainbow, is far too great for one human life to experience. And to run the risk of damaging the miraculous machinery we have been vouchsafed seems to me to be counterlife, counterproductive, counterenjoyment. The thought of having to give up control of one's life to a drug, to live in the thrall of a chemical, and to live only for that next fix, seems to me to be the worst kind of servitude—to be a slave until one dies of the substance one is a slave to. That is mind-expanding? I call that suicide. That's saying no to life in no uncertain terms. Anything that alters one's full consciousness of the miracle of life is saying no to life.

But we teach our children to say yes to life and the world and its wonders and opportunities. Yes, indeed! We teach them that life is a festival only to the wise. And that "every man [read person] is a divinity in disguise, a god playing the fool."

Why should we not say yes to life? Surely life is the most astonishing state in the vast universe. Life is natural on earth; we have found it nowhere else. Being human puts each of us in charge of his or her destiny on this incredible planet speeding through space on the great wheel of the Milky Way galaxy at one million miles an hour. And as the great galaxy in the mystery of space turns on its invisible axis, we rotate around our life-giving sun, turning as we do on our own slightly wobbly axis with our captive moon.

Think about it once in a while. We enjoy an occasional science-fiction story or motion picture, but nothing can equal the reality of our existence. Here we dwell on this tiny grain of sand among billions of other grains and stars, some of which are so large that if one were placed where our sun now resides, our planet would be almost in its exact center! And out of it all, we have this delightful blue planet, small but most agreeable, with its wonderful oceans and seas, its snow and glaciers and forbidding deserts and its very dwellable places in between. It boggles my mind! And in the midst of it all, we are granted a holiday on earth. How we tend to underestimate everything! How we look for a king to serve, before whom to fall on our knees in abject subjection! "Tell us what to do!" we shout. "Show us the way, lead us, we are sheep." "Poor little lambs who have lost our way, baa, baa, baa."

We need only to stand up and choose our first destination. We need to stop playing the fool. Aristotle said, "Excellence is an art won by training and habituation. We do not act rightly because we have virtue or excellence, but rather we have those qualities because we have acted rightly. We are what we repeatedly do. Excellence, then, is not an art but a habit."

"We are what we repeatedly do." But what we do is a matter of choice. Excellence is a habit. So are ordinary, common ways of doing things; so is a poor, substandard way of doing things. We form habits to match our outlook on life. Aristotle said, "We do not act rightly because we have virtue or excellence, but we rather have those because we have acted rightly." We are what we do and how we do what we do. But what we do and how we do what we do are matters of personal choice. We are the only creatures on earth with a choice as to what we do and how we do it.

Saying yes can lead us to excellence: "Yes, I will do that to the very best of my ability." Doing it well repeatedly will lead to the habit of excellence. Excellence is a wonderful way to say yes to life. Excellence invariably brings us joy. The distinguished philosopher George Santayana said, "There is no cure for birth and death save to enjoy the interval." Excellence helps us enjoy our days.

The distinguished Jesuit paleontologist Pierre Teilhard de Chardin said, "It is our duty as men and women to proceed as though difficulties do not exist. We are collaborators in creation."

Our own Henry David Thoreau put it this way: "We have only to proceed confidently in the direction of our dreams and live the life we have imagined to meet with a success unexpected in common hours."

Sometimes one wonders how many times we must be bludgeoned over the head with liberating truth before we can muster the confidence to stand up on our hind legs and build great lives for ourselves.

We must clean the slate of all of our pet myths, such as, "It takes money to make money." If that were true, we would have a world of poor people; rich people had to start somewhere. "You have to know someone." "You have to get the breaks." "You have to be lucky." God, how we love to surround our inactivity with nonsense of that kind!

Personally, I'd rather go along with the great ones. Don't talk, listen. Listen to that inner voice. You can't learn anything when you're talking.

I love the way James Allen put it in his classic little book, *As a Man Thinketh*:

> Dream lofty dreams, and as you dream, so shall you become. Your Vision is the promise of what you shall one day be; your Ideal is the prophecy of what you shall at last unveil.
>
> The greatest achievement was at first and for a time a dream. The oak sleeps in the acorn; the bird waits in the egg; and in the highest vision of the soul a waking angel stirs. Dreams are the seedlings of realities.
>
> You will realize the Vision (not the idle wish) of your heart, be it base or beautiful, or a mixture of both, for you will always gravitate toward that which you, secretly, most love. Into your hands will be placed the exact results of your own thoughts; you will receive that which you earn; no more, no less.

Saying yes to the world means we have balance and pretty good mental health. The Menninger Foundation recognizes some guidelines for good mental health.

To paraphrase the late Dr. William Menninger's criteria of emotional maturity: Check yourself against six points from those guidelines.

Six important attributes of mentally healthy people are:

1. A wide variety of sources of gratification. This does not mean that they chase frenetically from one activity to another but that they find pleasure in many different ways and from many

things. If, for any reason, they lose some of their sources of gratification, they have others to turn to. For example, a person who loses a good friend through death may sorrow, but if he has other good friends, he draws psychological sustenance from them and recovers. But if a person loses his only good friend, he has little to fall back on and continues to grieve in his loneliness. A person has the same problem if his only interest is his job, or his immediate family, or a single hobby.

2. Flexibility under stress. A windstorm may blow over a great oak, while the grass and reeds about it are undamaged. They are flexible; the oak is not. Mentally healthy people learn to roll with the punches. When faced with problems, they can see alternative solutions. Flexibility under stress is closely related to having a wide variety of sources of gratification. With more supports to fall back on, a person is less threatened by situations that produce fear and anxiety.

3. Recognition and acceptance of limitations and assets. Put another way, they have a reasonably accurate picture of themselves, and they like what they see. This does not mean they are complacent about themselves, but that they know they cannot be anyone else, and that's all right with them. They build on their assets and don't knock their heads against the wall in areas in which they have little or no ability.

4. Understanding the importance of treating people as individuals. Mentally healthy persons recognize others as distinct and different and original human beings and treat them as such— make them feel important and esteemed. People who are preoccupied with themselves pay only superficial attention to others. They are so tied up in themselves that they cannot observe the subtleties in another person's feelings, nor can they really listen. Mentally healthy people care about what other people feel.

5. Keeping active and productive. Mentally healthy people use their resources on their own behalf and on behalf of others. They do what they do because they like to do it and enjoy

using their skills. They do not feel driven to produce to prove themselves. They are in charge of their activities; the activities are not in charge of them. When they are chosen for leadership of one sort or another, it is because they have the skills to lead in a given situation, not because they have to exercise power over others.

6. The capacity to love.

Qualifying as a mentally healthy person isn't all that difficult, but it does include those six important criteria. Those who qualify are people who like to say yes to life and do so whenever they feel they can.

Do you have a wide variety of sources of gratification? Are you flexible under stress? Flexibility under stress was once nominated as the most important qualification of a great executive by the Harvard School of Business. Do you recognize and accept your limitations as well as your assets? Do you treat others as individuals, each one separate and worth recognition as such? Are you active and productive? Are you in the driver's seat of your activities rather than in the back seat, going along with someone else's direction? Are you capable of loving?

If you answered yes to all six of the criteria, you are no doubt the person I'm writing about in this book. Perhaps you're looking for a new aim, a new goal, a new interest in life. If you do not meet the six criteria, examine the one or ones that you do not meet, and resolve to qualify for it as soon as you can. And by all means, relax and open your doors and windows to the fresh breeze of life and its possibilities.

CHAPTER X

The Last Chapter

The Four Factors

For weeks I stewed over writing this chapter. I must have started it a dozen times, but each attempt ended in a kind of random wandering. Finally, one morning over coffee, it dawned upon me that I can't write the last chapter for you. You must do that. And I can't write the last chapter for me because I am in the process of living it. I've done many of the necessary things and formed some of the right habits, and now I'm in the process of coloring the final pages in my book.

What is perhaps most interesting is that I'm enjoying this chapter most of all. Of course that's the way it should be; surveys indicate that we tend to get happier as we grow older. People are happier at forty than they were at thirty; happier at fifty than they were at forty. I can certainly vouch for far greater happiness at sixty-one than at any other age of my life. I say sixty-one because that was my age when I met Diana, who flooded my life with sunshine and laughter.

Like many Americans, I had had trouble with the institution of marriage. My first marriage tottered along for eighteen years and the second for fourteen, so you can see I wasn't a fly-by-night sort of person. But after the end of the second, I vowed never to marry again—until and unless I found, and knew I'd found, the one and only. It took seven years! And it was worth every second of that time. I've been happier since meeting and marrying Diana—at this writing it's been just five years—than ever before in my life. Every day is a wonderful experience for both of us. We were kindred spirits orbiting about, waiting to come together.

Most of the time I knew I would meet Diana and that when I did, everything would fall into place in both our lives. That's exactly what happened.

Now, as we color the last section of our books together, we look forward to many years of joyous adventuring. It's a happy, colorful cap on our lives, for which we are endlessly grateful.

All my life, at just the right time—and not a second sooner—I have been blessed with the greatest good fortune. I've had my share of setbacks, but with steadily recurring faith that the system I've outlined in this book really works, I have watched it confirm and reconfirm itself over and over again.

Yes, we obtain what we make up our minds to obtain; we fulfill our expectations in each of the three vital areas of our lives: our work, our family, our income—and not necessarily, by any means, in that order.

I knew I wanted to be a writer when I was still a young boy. Broadcasting came along as a serendipitous spin-off. So my work has been satisfactorily progressing from the time I was mustered out of the Marine Corps following World War II. Since 1950, I have been writing and broadcasting my own radio programs. And since 1956, I've been writing and narrating recordings in an attempt to spread the word about achievement.

One of the most difficult ideas for the human being to fully assimilate is that although we are social creatures, achievement is an individual and isolated affair. That is, although we are a part of a population of many millions and must find our being in successful relationships with such numbers—in fact our success depends upon it—we must think and act as distinct and separate, even different, creatures in order to succeed in the steady pursuit of completion of our goals.

Just as a successful marriage, filled to overflowing with joy and genuine love for one another, depends on two distinct individuals whose characteristics and experience perfectly meld them into an even better whole, our success as individuals operating in a highly populated environment must be an individual thing in each of the three categories: family, work, and income.

We need all three. And keep in mind that income comes in two distinct and important categories: it's the money we earn for the service we render, and equally important, it's the psychic income we receive for the service we render and for the full or nearly full utilization of ourselves in the process. This psychic income comes from both the family and the work and results in our self-esteem, the way we feel about and accept ourselves.

We need all three, and we need both kinds of income.

A man without the right woman in his life is a crippled, truncated, incomplete person. The same is true for women. Each of us is a half, walking around looking for the other half. When the two correct halves finally come together, all the lights go on and the music swells and anything at all becomes quite possible.

And it's the same with the idea of work—or profession or career or whatever you want to call it. Two halves coming together make a whole. But just as a successful marriage is different from all other marriages, successful or not, a person and his or her work, when it's the correct work, are different from all others, even those in the same work. That's because no two people are alike, and each of them brings a slightly different chemistry and experience and genetic profile to whatever he or she does.

Diana and I were both married to other people before we met and fell deeply in love. Neither of us could bring to the others exactly what we brought to our relationship. Nor was it possible before, for either of us, to find the astonishing blend of characteristics that worked to our mutual benefit when we found one another. It was as if a master craftsman had formed two oddly shaped and complex parts and tossed them at different times into the Pacific Ocean thousands of miles apart. In each was the required electronic homing device that would seek its perfect counterpart but that in the attempt might first form imperfect connections with others similarly involved. Finally one morning, in a completely strange setting, these two complicated parts floated into each other's range and began a circling process to attempt, once again, to see if a perfect matchup was possible. And *click*—the two suddenly found they fit. Not perfectly at first, but very well. And with the passing of each day after that, the fit gets better and tighter until the seams are no longer visible. From that point on, each exists as part of a whole. They find their being together. The family is a success!

Work should be a similar phenomenon but with greater latitude. Mozart wrote great operas, but he also wrote delightful vaudeville sketches. As long as wonderfully original music was involved, Mozart was in his element.

An architect can design a dwelling or a great auditorium or a church or a child's treehouse—or a prison.

To find a mate we must know that the person exists and that, sooner or later, we will come in contact with that person. With such expectancy we become a willing magnet receptively set at the correct signal—a scanning radar, we might say—with the inchoate picture of the person we're looking for a part of our mind and being. We need then to bide our time and wait for the lights to go on and the music to play.

Finding and living in the right work is in some ways quite similar, except that it's a comfort, a competence that we don't feel when doing other things. We can all do hundreds of things. Just as we can meet hundreds of people of the opposite sex. But one of those things we can do with an uncommon ease and facility. The way Robinson Jeffers or Edgar Allan Poe could write poetry that moves us to tears. The way Walter Payton plays football. When that happens, the work is a success.

And when that happens it often follows that income, in both important categories, will take care of itself. But with these two great divisions of life now successfully accomplished, it's time for creative thinking.

When one thinks creatively, the rest of one's life is assured to be endlessly interesting and endlessly successful. For with creative thinking—which includes the input of others who join your team—you're on a roll, as they say in Las Vegas, that needs to end only when you do. And it often happens that it need not end even then but may be carried on by others.

To a happy home life, to the right work—whatever that happens to be, and it will always involve serving others because that's what we're here for—adding creative thinking will give us the endless tessellation of new goals to reach. We will have something interesting to do every day of our lives. And the days when we have nothing at all to do, the idle Sunday or holiday that we devote to leisure, will have meaning also because we've earned the time off and feel good about it. Millions are now enjoying their retirement years for the same reason—they've earned them, and each new day is an exercise in doing exactly what they want to do.

As I was writing this chapter in Carmel, California, the Federal Express courier arrived. She's a delightful, attractive young woman of perhaps twenty-six or -seven with whom we'd had a happy relationship for many months. I asked her if she enjoyed her work with Federal Express.

"I love it," she said. I think we had known that by the energetic and cheerful way she delivers and picks up letters and packages.

I commented on the hundreds of young women and men who have found meaningful employment because Federal Express has come into being. Whereupon our young courier invited us to attend a Federal Express open–house party on an upcoming Thursday evening in Watsonville, a town a few miles north of us.

"We're hoping Fred Smith will come," she said.

"Who is Fred Smith?" I asked.

"He's the man who started Federal Express," she said, obviously surprised that I didn't know. "We've invited him. I hope he's not too busy."

Fred Smith! I thought. What an ordinary name for the man who created a whole new world of mail and package delivery. What an astonishing and talented person he must be. I hope he's as successful in his family life as he is in his work. Think of the hundreds of thousands, the millions his fertile imagination has served! And to think we didn't even know we needed Federal Express until Fred Smith put his beautiful system to work! Now there are thousands of jobs, where before there was only a vacuum—jobs for pilots and ground personnel, jobs manufacturing millions of dollars in equipment, and jobs for all the cheerful, energetic pickup and delivery people like that happy young woman who serves us. The prosperity radiating from such an enterprise is incalculable. I hope Fred Smith made it to the Watsonville opening.

Federal Express is a good example of the positive effects a

good idea, put into action, can bring about. And what a perfect example of creative thinking! Letter and package delivery is one of the world's oldest businesses, and airmail is as old as aviation. But door-to-door overnight mail from any two points in the country was a new idea whose time had definitely arrived. It was an idea the U.S Postal Service should have thought of, but creative thinking and monopolies have never worked well together. They're incompatible and don't attract the same kind of people.

How about you and what you do? How can creative thinking revolutionize your work?

On a scale of one to ten how do you score each category—work, incomes of both kinds, and family—of your life? Mine has tens at every level, I'm happy to say, but of course I've been at it for some time. I love my work, my incomes are just what I want them to be, and my family life couldn't be better. I don't intend to stop here, but for the present I'm on schedule. The goals I have yet to achieve are in order and are coming closer all the time. Ten years from now I expect I'll look back on this time much as I look at snapshots now that were taken ten years ago—fondly perhaps, but with no desire to turn back the clock. It's getting better all the time.

Let's add creative thinking as a fourth factor. Our list now reads:

WORK
INCOME (psychic and financial)
FAMILY
THINKING

I think I can hear someone saying, "I'm not much of a creative thinker." You don't have to be much of a creative thinker to come up with one idea!

When someone succeeds, everybody benefits. The entire community and the nation benefit, and in time, the whole world can benefit. Think of the countless things that did not exist in the past from which you benefit every day. Each of them was a good idea, and good ideas are free. Implementing them may cost a great deal of money. A good idea attracts money. The better the idea, the more money it attracts.

Form the habit of using a legal pad and pen. Jot down your ideas, especially those that affect you emotionally—those ideas with which you want to personally become involved. Recently I received a letter from a woman in New Orleans who for many years has been deeply affected by the community's treatment of stray and unwanted pets and domestic animals. She said she had joined the SPCA and had donated funds to help the problem but felt that her efforts were inadequate to do much about what is, for her and for millions like her, a pressing national disgrace. One day she got the idea that a television series "of the M*A*S*H* type, centered around the care and protection of animals" would help provide an ongoing crusade of the kind she wanted to bring about.

Of course, there are no "M*A*S*H* type" television programs. M*A*S*H* was and is unique; it stands alone, a marvelous example of excellent writing and acting with an important theme: the absurdity and bloodshed of war. But I knew what she meant, and I agreed with her. I wrote to her that it was up to her to get some scripts written and to get in touch with the right people. An idea with no substance to it, with nothing one can hold in one's hands and rub against one's brains is just that, an idea and no more. Its value depends upon its implementation and demands the rolling up of sleeves, midnight oil, and perspiration. But that's fun, too, when you're on the track of something big and worthwhile.

It takes, as I have outlined earlier, one hundred percent commitment. There is no success without risk; remember that balancing bar. There's more success lurking in intelligent risk than in all the so-called "safe" jobs in the world. The world is full of people quite willing to toss out an idea, as long as they are not involved in the work or the financial risk. A man wrote to me some years back, "I have an excellent idea, Mr. Nightingale, if you would be willing to write the book about it." I told him that if he really had a great idea, the words would come to him and he could write his own book. It's true: when we have something to say, the words are there for us.

Another time, following a speech in which I had used notes to stay on track and remember to say all I wanted to say, a man came up to me and said, "Would you mind giving me your notes for that speech?"

I looked at him in amazement. Those notes were the culmination of decades of study and research and the result of careful organization. I had spent hours on them just the night before. And he wanted me to hand them to him, just like that! I suggested, as kindly as I could, that his speeches should reflect his own scholarship and ideas. And when I asked him if he had taken notes during my talk, which I had noticed many people in the audience doing, he shook his head. "Sorry, I didn't have anything to write on."

He was like a hitchhiker to whom I once gave a free fifty-mile ride from Santa Cruz to Monterey, California. Before getting out of the car he said, "Do you think you could spare five dollars?"

I said, "No, I can't spare five dollars, but I do have a good idea: I'm not going to charge you anything for the fifty-mile ride in my beautiful, air-conditioned car. How about that?" To which he mumbled something and failed to close my door completely.

During the speech I'd given from the notes that the man wanted me to give him, I had given him all the ideas necessary to solve most of his problems. Apparently all of that had sailed over his head, and he had visions of himself ululating my speech from my notes—a free ride. But was it free? It seems to me the so-called free riders in life pay an exorbitant price, indeed.

We don't have to say *creative* thinking anymore. All thinking tends to be creative. The word *creative* seems to frighten a lot of people. It seems to take on the connotation of other creative endeavors, such as music, painting, or poetry. Thinking is something we come abundantly equipped to do, and we can all do it to our own satisfaction and to the satisfaction of who knows how many others, as it pertains to what we are uniquely equipped to do.

If you are happy in your present work, stay in it. You can find all the creative possibilities you need within it. If you are a homemaker, the possibilities are endless. If you want to find creative expression outside of your work, in an avocation or hobby, fine. But utilize your strengths, and they begin with your mind. As Thomas J. Watson of IBM used to say, "THINK." Look what thinking did for IBM.

Epilogue

A Nice Balance

Who succeeds in America, and why?

The person who succeeds in America is the person who sets his or her own wages, goals, and lifestyle. Successful people are those who discover that life is ready and willing to meet their requirements. They set their incomes to meet their needs and wants by discovering within themselves a marketable factor and developing that factor to whatever degree necessary in order to derive the appropriate reward response.

Unsuccessful people are those who make their lifestyles fit whatever wages they receive. They put themselves on the receiving end of things and have little to say about their own economic welfare.

Successful people put themselves behind the wheel of their lives; the unsuccessful ride in the passenger seats.

Almost everything has an economic base today. We are rewarded by the amount of money we receive for what we do. What we do in a free society, and what we charge for what we do in a free society, are largely matters of personal choice.

If we discover our best opportunities for personal expression are within the framework of a large corporation, we can so develop and apply ourselves as to reach whatever levels of accomplishment and reward we are willing to reach.

It takes time to succeed—and it should. We need to earn our stripes through the daily passage of time and experience so that each successive step is accepted and applauded by those who have come to know us. Meaningful and richly rewarding journeys take time. They take preparation and careful planning, and—as every seasoned traveler knows—they are subject to the vagaries of incident and the mistakes and inefficiencies of others along the way. But although the journey has its adventures and misadventures, it also has a definite upward momentum, and there is no doubting its eventual destination—the goal of the person in command. Each new upward step along the way prepares our resolute traveler for the next plateau. And if he or she does not lose the exciting vision of the goal to be reached or meet with an untimely end (the silent tragedy of war and accident), the goal, with all the trimmings and more, will be his or hers.

Remember Cervantes's words, "The journey is better than the inn." The journey is our life, our holiday on earth, our time here, as we successively set new goals or dive back into our great rivers of interest—or both!

We receive what we fully expect to receive—and usually a good deal more. We become what we think about.

We become successful to the extent of our true desires and determination. And we do so by building on our strong point, our forte.

What is your forte? You should know what it is by now. At what are you best? What gives you the most, the deepest satisfaction? Whatever that is can be honed to marketable proportions in some way and applied in service to others to earn you the rewards you seek and should have and will have.

And that's your part of the bargain. No one is supposed to do that for you, or hold your hand, or rush to your aid every time you slip or fall back a little. That's the earning part that falls on each of us. There is help enough on every side if we are wise enough and energetic enough to make use of it—help in the form of books or recorded cassette programs such as those produced by my company. And there are the numerous people who come to our aid once we're on course. But such people need not be sought or importuned. They come of their own natural need, like magic, at just the right time. Events begin to fall into our lives like missing pieces of a jigsaw puzzle. Such good fortune is the mark of a person with the attitude that tells the world that he or she knows where he or she is going and fully expects to get there. They approach their commitments "with intentionality and delight," as my friend Dr. Charles Garfield puts it in his book and cassette program, *Peak Performance.*

The distinguished Dr. Abraham Maslow put it this way: "If you deliberately plan to be less than you are capable of being, then I warn you that you will be unhappy for the rest of your life. You'll be evading your own capacities, your own possibilities."

And let me add this: If you think you can succeed in a large way and play it safe at the same time, you are sadly mistaken. Success takes risk; it takes full commitment. You go out on a limb, so to speak, and take your chances alone. The warm, comfortable, huddling masses must be left behind along with the old neighborhood and the small dreams. *Risk* and *success* are at opposite ends of the same balancing beam. You cannot have one without the corresponding weight of the other. Risk ups the ante, raises the greens fee, and limits the membership. But it makes playing more fun, and you seldom have to wait in line anymore.

The late motion–picture producer Mike Todd put it well. He said, "Being broke is a temporary situation; being poor is a state of mind."

Who has success in America? Or in Canada, Mexico, or Peru, or in France or West Germany or Japan? Or anywhere else? Those who have taken charge of their lives and are directing them to their own best use.

Who does not have success? Those persons who have not taken charge of the direction of their lives but have simply reacted to the environment in which they found themselves. They have become a part of it.

Our environment, at any stage of our lives, is a mirrorlike reflection of ourselves at that time. It may be a transitional stage or, as is more often the case, a permanent statement of ourselves and the extent of our preparation and contribution.

But what about the millions of women whose financial incomes and lifestyles are to a considerable extent determined by the men they have married? Once again, it's the result of a decision on the woman's part. She need not cast her financial lot in life on the ability or ambition of her husband. She has an excellent mind of her own and is free at all times, married or single, to make her own decisions. She can be of enormous help to the marriage partnership by adding her own intelligence, creativity, and talents to the service side. Hundreds of thousands of wives, perhaps millions, are responsible for much, if not most or even all, of the family's success. Women tend to be more practical than men. They also tend to have a better balance between the right and left hemispheres of the brain: high creativity and sound, practical balance. My life, my world, would be a sadly crippled affair without my wife Diana's contribution, in every facet of our lives together.

It often happens at public affairs where I am to be the speaker that because of my life's work, I receive a disproportionate share of the limelight. When I introduce Diana as my wife, I want to tell everyone in attendance—as if I could—how much more she is to me and to our lives together than the familiar word wife implies. As I told her one day recently, she is to my life what the sun is to the earth. To ask what share she deserves in our success since our marriage is to ask the impossible. I couldn't have done it without her. She makes it all worthwhile and so much fun. She brings her solid intelligence to bear on all that we do, and her marvelous sense of humor and quick laughter and response are endlessly charming and endearing.

The old cliché, "Behind every successful man there is a good woman," is as ridiculous as it is patronizing. It's as ridiculous as saying, "Behind every man who has failed to be all that he can be is a woman who has failed." There are often wonderful women who share, without complaint, the failures of their husbands, just as there are silly idiotic women behind many successful men and vice versa.

The fact is that men and women come in all possible permutations of the species, and there are no good guidelines or explanations of why certain men marry certain women or vice versa. But rules for achievement have nothing whatever to do with gender. They apply as well and as disinterestedly to women as they do to men: As we sow, so shall we reap. If you want a true assessment of the extent of your service to your fellow human beings, consider the extent of your rewards. You may be underpaid, it's true, but if you accept underpayment, that is your compromise.

If a woman feels she's missing too much of life because she is married to an under- or overachiever, she should have married someone with whom she shared a great deal in common—including goals. And if you're not happy with your mate's progress and achievement, how about adding your own? What can you do to help or even solve the problem? What's your forte? Are you making the best use of it? How much of yourself have you brought into full development?

People see a successful person living the good life with all the perquisites of modern success and say, "Look at that! Man, would I love to have what he, or she, has. How lucky can you get!"

Lucky? Luck is what happens when preparedness meets opportunity. People who say such things don't know about the planning, the study, the preparation, the long hours, the hard work, and the steady, implacable resolve. All they see is the end result, and they call it luck.

Many years ago when I had my own daily radio and television programs on WGN in Chicago, a friend of mine, the sales manager of a Chicago radio station, told me an interesting story at lunch one day. It was about an incident that had occurred the week before at his country club. He had been playing a round of golf with his regular foursome. The tee of one of the holes was contiguous to a main highway. As the foursome approached the tee, they saw a semitrailer rig grind to a stop alongside the tee and a large driver climb down from the cab and lean on the fence—just a few feet from the tee—to watch them hit their tee shots.

Golfers grow accustomed to other members of the club watching them tee off, especially on the first tee, where there is often a group of members getting ready to play. But this was different. There was hostility crackling in the air as the truck driver looked at the four middle-aged men playing a round of golf on a weekday.

It turned out to be my friend Bill's honor, so he walked to the tee markers, teed up his ball, then stood behind it, sighting down the fairway and taking a couple of easy practice swings. He was trying desperately to regain his concentration. There was no sound from the intently observing truck driver. Bill took his stance, waggled his three wood—a wise choice, under the circumstances—and then, after sighting once again down the fairway, he shot a quick glance at the truck driver. Whereupon the truck driver said, in a loud, clear voice, "Go on! Hit it, you rich son of a bitch!"

And my friend Bill swung his three wood with all the force and power he could muster. The badly topped ball dribbled off the tee. Bill had lost his cool.

"And the tragedy of it all," Bill said that day at lunch, "was that I'm not rich!"

How many times in the discomfort of his post-flub imagination had Bill seen himself hit the best shot of his life—one of those great high arcers—far and away down the center of the fairway as the astonished truck driver looked on with open-mouthed admiration before slouching back to the cab of his truck?

Bill was a typical businessman golfer and a hardworking sales manager. After the truck driver left, following Bill's failure in the spotlight, Bill's friends insisted that he hit a Mulligan. They agreed that the leering truck driver was a factor that might have ruined any one of their shots. Besides, he wasn't a natural hazard and as such could be removed before taking the next shot.

But a very interesting story lurks in that incident. Once the truck driver made his outrageous statement, Bill assumed the role of an imposter. He should have backed off before hitting his shot and walked over to the truck driver. He might have said, "My name is Bill Randall [the name is fictitious]. I am not a rich man—far from it. I'm a hardworking radio–station sales manager trying to enjoy a round of golf with some friends. Now if you'll shut up, I'll do my best to make a decent shot."

Then, after setting the record straight, comfortably back in his true identity, chances are Bill would have hit one of his better drives. But Bill, who is of a generation that often viewed rich men in much the same way as the truck driver had, did not refute the "rich son of a bitch" comment and thus had to fail on the shot. He had to show the "rich son of a bitch" in a bad light. And he did.

Had Bill been a rich man and comfortable in the role, he would have hit a good drive, ignoring the truck driver and his rude comment as he might ignore a waiter clearing away the dishes after a business luncheon.

We tend to perform well in the role in which we habitually see ourselves. That's another reason goals are so important. When we seriously establish a difficult goal, we immediately begin to become the person to whom such an achievement would naturally accrue. Bill did not see himself—and had never seen himself—as a rich man. He saw himself in the role he lived, as a sales manager for a big-city radio station, working toward retirement. Bill was successful and content in his role.

He may have idly wished from time to time that he were a rich man, just as the woman wished she could play the piano as beautifully as the visiting concert pianist. But wishes aren't serious goals to which people fully commit themselves. Separating wishes from serious goals is the mark of maturity, and we must be willing to pay the price.

Is It Worth It?

Is success, as we've defined it here, worth the trouble, the effort, the commitment, the dedication, the perseverance? Yes. Yes, of course it is worth it. The time will pass anyway; why not put it to constructive, productive use? Everyone benefits, nobody loses.

In the field of human endeavor, it's the successful men and women who make the important difference. They see growth and improvement as the natural order of things, and they can see themselves growing into new arenas of achievement and commensurate reward.

"Only that day dawns to which we are awake," wrote Henry Thoreau.

What a pity it is for a human being with the gift of consciousness to take life and all that is connected with life for granted—to live each day as his or her due and quite likely find more to criticize than to be grateful for. Yet that is exactly how millions live out their lives. They often give the impression that they have a contract with forever when it is really for only a handful of years. Why not give it all we have to give? Why not make a thorough exploration of ourselves and by so doing find what it is we have to add to the quality somewhere? To make life better because we made an appearance here; to serve in the way we think we can serve best.

Succeeding is so much fun! Especially if it means moving several levels above the one where you spent your youth. For one thing it tells you you have done a better job of serving the community than your parents. That's progress. Perhaps your children will do a better job of it than you and keep the ball rolling.

Succeeding brings so much of the world within the realm of experience for you. You can actually fly on the *Concorde* and take a trip on the *Orient Express*, cruise along the coast of China if you like, or fly over the poles. Succeeding brings the world within range, including much greater success.

Now—let's think in new directions.

How about this idea? Fly to Cannes, France. After a few days on the Riviera, charter a yacht and spend the next couple of months exploring the coasts of Italy and Yugoslavia and the Greek islands. After making arrangements to charter the boat again next year to continue your explorations, fly back home and devote nine or ten months to business. Then, back to Europe and your leisurely explorations: Turkey, Israel, Egypt. After visiting Cairo for a while, how about sailing up the Nile? Two or three months each summer exploring the perimeter of the Mediterranean would still leave nine months or so each year for important work. That's a nice balance. Or, on your leisurely explorations, whenever you find a spot you especially like, just stay there as long as you like—spend the whole summer there if you like. No packing and unpacking, no fiddling with luggage and transfers. Just check in with customs at each new country. American dollars are welcome everywhere. And in your resting time, time spent on deck relaxing, you might want to get out the old yellow pad and make a few notes. Good ideas can be wooed anywhere. Just think—one idea that you might get early one morning while sailing in the Adriatic or the Aegean Sea could be worth millions when properly put to work back home. It might pay for the whole summer many times over. Remember, it isn't the time you spend working that matters as much as the good ideas you come up with and then put into operation. Besides, with nine months out of the year for productive effort, three months of leisure should produce dozens of excellent ideas. Ideas find leisure time the best soil in which to grow and show their bright, intriguing faces above ground. Taking three months off each year could be more productive than the traditional three weeks—more fun, too. If you need to go back for any reason for a few days or a week, there are always airports nearby.

Let's say chartering the yacht costs two thousand dollars a week, including crew and cook, and you charter for twelve weeks. That's about twenty-five thousand dollars, plus extras, for the summer, plus air fare. Not bad. A lot cheaper than buying the yacht and having to maintain it and insure it year 'round. In fact, you could go on doing that for ten years or so and still save tons of money over what it would cost to buy and maintain your own boat. Besides, if you can't come up with the twenty-five-thousand-dollar idea in three months of floating around the Mediterranean, you're not thinking at all. Just don't forget to pack that yellow legal pad and a few good ballpoint pens. You might look for a yacht named *Eureka!* Surely somewhere in Greece....

We tend to perform well in the role in which we habitually see ourselves. Cruising around the Mediterranean could do wonders for your self-image. Who knows, you might find just the spot to build the loveliest little European-style American retirement village—with all European capital. Well, there's just no end to the good ideas that some leisurely world travel might engender. Wandering around small, offbeat villages, who knows what we might see or pick up in the way of an unusual product that might go over big back in the States?

And just for the hell of it, let's say that chartering the yacht costs *twice* twenty-five thousand dollars; that it costs you fifty thousand dollars a summer. You could still charter every summer for ten years and save money over what it would cost to own and maintain your own yacht.

There's only one good reason to own your own yacht, if that's what you would rather do. If owning your own yacht is important to you and you don't mind the annual hauling, scraping, and painting and the zillions of things that go wrong on a yacht and have to be repaired and the registration and the insurance and the rest of it, then by all means own your own yacht or your own airplane or RV or whatever. Because it's important that you do what you most want to do with the rewards you've earned from the service you've performed or provided. Besides, everybody needs his or her toy, and that's when what is practical has no place whatever in the picture. There are times to be impractical, too.

I brought up the idea of cruising the coasts of the Mediterranean because I wanted to move your mind laterally, away from the ordinary. It's important that we think in new directions from time to time. The more often, the better. Genius has been defined as "the ability to think in new directions." After all, wasn't that what typified all the great geniuses you can think of? The great artists, composers, writers, inventors—they were all inventors, all creators, they all thought in new directions.

Life should be many things for all of us, but it should seldom if ever be boring. We don't have enough time to waste any of it in a state of boredom, or at least any more than we have to. It may be necessary for us to attend meetings, but hopefully they can be kept as short and as close to the actual agenda as good manners permit. Even meetings can be made more interesting with a bit of preparation and originality.

In her marvelous book, *The Aquarian Conspiracy*, Marilyn Ferguson writes, "If we are not learning and teaching we are not awake and alive. Learning is not only like health, it *is* health."

One can be just as bored sitting in the cockpit of a yacht anchored in the harbor at Portofino as one can sitting in one's office in New York City at three o'clock on a Friday afternoon. But not if one is learning and teaching. Then boredom is never present. If you are at all like me, you require learning and teaching just about every day. I call it "doing some work," but learning and teaching are what it amounts to, in my case reading and writing (teaching). I need to know that I have done something worthwhile in order to fully enjoy my leisure time or a weekend. Perhaps that's the result of forty years of working, but for me there must be a balance of work and play—both to be fully enjoyed. I will never reach the age when I am no longer interested in learning or in putting what I have learned into language that others can understand, enjoy, and pass along. That seems to be my forte.

What are the odds that a person, following the guidelines of this program, will actually succeed? I would say his chances of failure are virtually nonexistent. The odds are overwhelmingly in one's favor; in fact, there's nothing else one can do but succeed! It's all in the goal and the planning that precede the establishment of that goal, if the person is a Goal Person. If the person is a River Person, he or she is automatically a success as long as he or she is swimming in that river.

It's like asking what the odds are that a person who has made up his or her mind to become a professional chef will actually become a professional chef. What else can that person become? Keep in mind that we're talking about people who are fully committed.

Remember the comment, "The American people can become anything they decide to become. The trouble is...they seldom make that decision."

I woke up one morning about fifteen minutes before the clock-radio alarm was to sound off. It was a great experience just to lie back and luxuriate. There popped into my mind the thought that life is its own reward. It came to me that having life itself, life being such a miraculous achievement, is like winning the grand prize. What we do after that—what we do with our lives—is the frosting on the cake.

We hear young people ask, "What is the purpose of life?" The purpose of life is service and whatever we decide to do or be to provide that service. We can do whatever we want with it. That is the terrible (to me, wonderful) freedom of the Existentialists.

Never before have I been as conscious of how stunning an achievement life itself is, in all its forms. Perhaps that was how the great Dr. Albert Einstein felt about life and why he was so reverent about it in all its multifarious forms. We're so lucky to actually experience life, to be given the opportunity to do something worthwhile for others as our way of earning our way here, just as they spend their days serving us in so many ways. It becomes important then for us to do our work as creatively, as excellently as we can, and to think of new and better ways to do those things that it has been given us to do, so that we can maximize our input during the time we spend working.

I remember reading something about what an ongoing education will do for us. That it teaches us to love what doesn't cost much, to love the sunrise and the sunset and the beating of the rain on roof and windows and the gentle fall of snow on a winter day.

The article went on to say that a good education teaches us to love life for its own sake. That's what I realized that morning when I woke up before the alarm sounded.

Being alive, just being alive, makes us winners. From then on, anything we want to add to the achievement is up to us. It needn't be a lot in the eyes of the world, but we can find our place in the scheme of things and do our thing—make our contribution whatever it happens to be.

One morning recently, Diana and I were in Hawaii. It was five o'clock and still pitch dark, but the sky was clear and filled with stars. We put on our bathing suits and walked out into the water until it was up to our shoulders. We put our arms around each other and drank in the clean warm breeze and luxuriated in the sea, now warm to our bodies. And as we watched, the sky in the east grew softly lighter until the great, craggy old volcanic mountains were clearly outlined against the early morning sky. What a joy it was— what a joy it is—just to be alive!

> If one advances confidently in the direction of his dreams, and endeavors to live the life he has imagined, he will meet with a success unexpected in common hours.
>
> Henry David Thoreau

Index

179